Log Cabin Quilts

New Quilts from an Old Favorite

LOG CABIN QUILTS

New Quilts from an Old Favorite

Edited by Victoria Faoro

American Quilter's Society

P.O. Box 3290, Paducah, KY 42003-3290

Dedication

This book is dedicated to quiltmakers
of all times and all places, whose works
continue to inspire and delight.

Exhibitions

DOUBLE WEDDING RING QUILTS: NEW QUILTS FROM AN OLD FAVORITE
1994 CONTEST

Museum of the American Quilter's Society, Paducah, Kentucky, April 16 – August 20, 1994
QuiltFest USA, Louisville, Kentucky, August 27 – 29, 1994
New England Quilt Museum, Lowell, Massachusetts, January 6, 1995 – February 2, 1995
Potsdam Public Museum, Potsdam, New York, March 1, 1995 – April 15, 1995
Edward-Dean Museum of Decorative Arts, Cherry Valley, California, April 30 – June 25, 1995
Dunedin Fine Art Center, Dunedin, Florida, June 30 – August 25, 1995

LOG CABIN QUILTS: NEW QUILTS FROM AN OLD FAVORITE
1995 CONTEST

Museum of the American Quilter's Society, Paducah, Kentucky, March 4 – June 3, 1995
Octagon Center for the Arts, Ames, Iowa, June 11 – August 6, 1995
Topeka & Shawnee Co. Public Museum, Topeka, Kansas, July 12 – August 31, 1996

Please reconfirm dates with the institutions.

For a current exhibition schedule or to schedule a booking, write
MAQS
PO Box 1540
Paducah, KY 42002-1540

Table of Contents

FOREWORD _____ 8

THE SPONSORS _____ 9

THE CONTEST _____ 10

THE WINNERS AND THEIR QUILTS _____ 12

    Inclined Log Cabin – *Keiko Goke* _____ 14

    Quasars – *Laura Murray* _____ 16

    Supernova 1994 – *Barbara T. Kaempfer* _____ 18

    Under the Log Cabin Sky – *Ann Fahl* _____ 20

    Elvis and the Penguins – *Nancy S. Brown* _____ 22

    Eye of the Storm – *Deanna D. Dison* _____ 24

    The Girls at Home – *Michele M. Duell* _____ 26

    Skylights – *Caryl Bryer Fallert* _____ 28

    Exuberance – *Wanda S. Hanson* _____ 30

    Just Because – *Barbara Oliver Hartman* _____ 32

    Spellbound – *Allison Lockwood* _____ 34

    Four and Twenty Blackbirds
    Divided by Two – *Catherine McIntee* _____ 36

    Butterflies Are Free – *Lois Monieson* _____ 38

    Geese in the Barn – *Charlotte Roach* _____ 40

    Raising a "New Age" Barn – *Cynthia Smith* _____ 42

    Log Cabin Squared – *Nancy Taylor* _____ 44

    Cabins in the Willows – *Diane Turscak* _____ 46

    Homage to Mondriaan VII:
      a GREEN QUILT – *Meiny Vermaas-van der Heide* _____ 48

LOG CABIN PATTERNS _____ 50

    6" Block _____ 52

    8" Block _____ 53

    10" Block _____ 54

12" Block _____ 56

14" Block _____ 58

WORKING WITH THE DESIGN – Tips & Techniques _____ 61

Adding Beading to Quilts *by Cynthia Smith* _____ 61

Free-form Patchwork: Making a Log Cabin Rose *by Ann Fahl* ____ 62

Achieving a Flat, Heirloom Look
   by Meiny Vermaas-van der Heide _____ 64

Catty-wampus Log Cabin *by Caryl Bryer Fallert* _____ 66

Free-pieced Designs *by Keiko Goke* _____ 67

Adding Checkerboard Strips and Couching
   by Barbara Oliver Hartman _____ 68

Creating Fabric Portraits *by Nancy S. Brown* _____ 70

Raw-edge Appliqué *by Michele M. Duell* _____ 72

PATTERNS FROM THE QUILTS _____ 73

Making Geese in the Barn *by Charlotte Roach* _____ 73

Butterflies Are Free *by Lois Monieson* _____ 76

Making "Exuberant" Log Cabin Blocks *by Wanda S. Hanson* _____ 80

Foundation Piecing *by Allison Lockwood* _____ 82

Log Cabin Squared *by Nancy Taylor* _____ 86

Eye of the Storm *by Deanna D. Dison* _____ 89

Combining Fabrics and Log Cabin Patterns
   by Diane Turscak _____ 97

Supernova *by Barbara T. Kaempfer* _____ 99

Quasars *by Laura Murray* _____ 103

Four and Twenty Blackbirds Divided by Two
   by Catherine McIntee _____ 105

INDEX OF QUILTMAKERS _____ 108

INDEX OF QUILTS _____ 109

THE MUSEUM _____ 110

Foreword

This book has been developed in conjunction with an annual Museum of the American Quilter's Society (MAQS) contest and exhibit entitled "New Quilts from Old Favorites." Dedicated to honoring today's quilter, MAQS has created this contest to recognize and share with others the fascinating array of interpretations that can grow out of a single traditional quilt pattern.

A brief introduction to the contest is followed by a presentation of the 18 finalists, including the five winners of awards. Full-color photographs of the quilts are accompanied by their makers' comments, which provide fascinating insights. Full-size templates for the traditional pattern enable anyone to make a Log Cabin quilt, minus the trouble of having to draft the templates needed. The tips, techniques, and patterns contributed by the winning contestants make a wide range of quilts easier to execute in fabric.

It is our hope that this combination of outstanding quilts, full-size patterns, and instructional information will inspire as many outstanding quilts as the original contest did – adding new contributions to this pattern's continuing tradition.

For information about entering the current year's contest write:

MAQS

PO Box 1540

Paducah, KY 42002-1540

The Sponsors

A special thanks goes to the corporations whose generous support has made this contest, exhibit, and book possible:

FABRIC TRADITIONS

Fairfield
Quality Polyester Products for Home and Industry

NEW HOME JANOME

The Contest

This publication grows out of an annual international contest sponsored by the Museum of the American Quilter's Society. Entitled "New Quilts from Old Favorites," this contest encourages quiltmakers to develop innovative quilts using a different traditional pattern each year. The theme for 1995 was the traditional Log Cabin pattern, a long-time favorite for both individuals and the producers of commercial patterns.

The only design requirement for quilts entered in the contest was that the quilt be recognizable in some way as related to the Log Cabin pattern. The quilt also had to be a minimum of 50" in each dimension and not exceed 100" in any one dimension, and it had to be quilted. A quilt could only be entered by the person who made it, and had to have been completed after December 31, 1989. Many exciting interpretations of this traditional pattern were submitted by quilters from around the world. From these entries were selected the 18 quilts featured in both this publication and the traveling exhibition.

The Log Cabin pattern, with its narrow interlocking "logs," has long been a favorite with quiltmakers. It is likely that the pattern was developed with an eye to using up narrow strips and other fabric scraps not appropriate for cutting squares and triangles. Working with this block, a quilter is able to combine and "organize" visually a very diverse group of fabrics. And when individual blocks are put together with one side pieced in light fabrics and the other in dark fabrics, dramatic overall designs can be created when the blocks are combined to create a quilt top.

Log Cabin

Contemporary quiltmakers were no less inspired than their predecessors by this pattern selected for the 1995 contest.

In some cases the quilts entered in this contest were projects that had already been underway at the time the contest was announced; in other cases they had already been completed.

A number of quilts entered in the competition were inspired by the contest theme. Many quilters commented that they had made Log Cabin quilts, but this was their first use of the pattern in an innovative way. This contest provided just the incentive they needed.

In at least one case the pattern is one that the quiltmaker has been exploring for a period of time, and several winners have remarked that they have found the Log Cabin pattern so interesting that they anticipate making other quilts based on this design. In this book you will find comments from each of the winners, illustrating the variety of experiences and reactions these individuals had to working with this popular traditional pattern.

Some of the quilters have retained much from the traditional design, modifying only slightly the pieced structure and usual use of the design. Other quilters have boldly moved in new directions, re-interpreting the design quite dramatically. The quilts are a wonderful reminder of the latitude that traditional patterns offer quiltmakers. These patterns are there to be followed to whatever degree the maker wishes. And regardless of the degree of modification, the results can be very spectacular.

The Winners

KEIKO GOKE
Sendai, Miyagi, Japan
INCLINED LOG CABIN

LAURA MURRAY
Minneapolis, Minnesota
QUASARS

BARBARA T. KAEMPFER
Mettmenstetten, Switzerland
SUPERNOVA 1994

ANN FAHL
Racine, Wisconsin
UNDER THE LOG CABIN SKY

NANCY S. BROWN
Oakland, California
ELVIS AND THE PENQUINS

And Their Quilts

DEANNA D. DISON

MICHELE M. DUELL

CARYL BRYER FALLERT

WANDA S. HANSON

BARBARA OLIVER HARTMAN

ALLISON LOCKWOOD

CATHERINE MCINTEE

LOIS MONIESON

CHARLOTTE ROACH

CYNTHIA SMITH

NANCY TAYLOR

DIANE TURSCAK

MEINY VERMAAS-VAN DER HEIDE

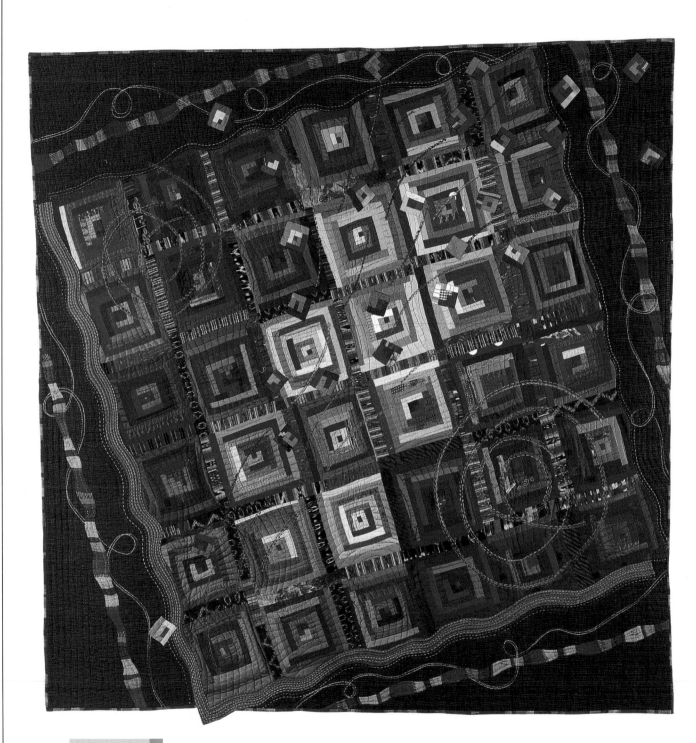

INCLINED LOG CABIN

70" x 70", 1992

Cottons, embroidery & Sachiko threads

Machine pieced, hand quilted,

embroidered & appliquéd

Keiko Goke

SENDAI, MIYAGI, JAPAN

MY QUILTMAKING

Since I chanced upon an article on patchwork quilts in a Japanese interior design magazine about 24 years ago, I have been making quilts. Friends from school are surprised because when I was a student I actually hated to sew. Now, every day I do needlework. However, I'm not conscious that I'm doing needlework. I feel that I'm actually painting; my needle is a paint brush and the fabrics become my paints.

When I began, I made traditional American patterns, but later I started making pictorial quilts and other different quilts. Fifteen years ago I opened Quilt Circle Kei. At the time there was interest in patchwork quilts, but there were few quilt schools in Japan. I was self-taught in quiltmaking, but felt I could teach what I had learned, and I also find it more enjoyable to work with friends.

Circle Kei members now number thirty, and many of us win prizes in competitions. I look forward to continuing to make quilts with my group members.

MY LOG CABIN QUILT

I have been making quilts for many years. As I work with various fabrics gathered around me, I look at them, and an idea of how the next quilt could be made comes to me.

What is perhaps most unusual about this quilt is that it was made without templates. To begin with, I made the 25 Log Cabin blocks in the center. Then I sewed together the pieced blocks and incorporated appropriate borders to adjust the overall size. I planned to finish with the quilt at that point, but when it was done I found I wanted to spice up. It was not as interesting visually as I wanted. I then decided to set the pieced section on point, and add four triangles.

In the beginning I worried about whether quiltmaking would go well without any templates. This was a very free way to work and I wasn't certain it would be suitable for me. I now recommend every quilter try working without templates. It is a very enjoyable way to work.

I love the Log Cabin design. I have made many quilts inspired by this challenging pattern, and I am sure that I'll make many more.

See page 67 for a design tip.

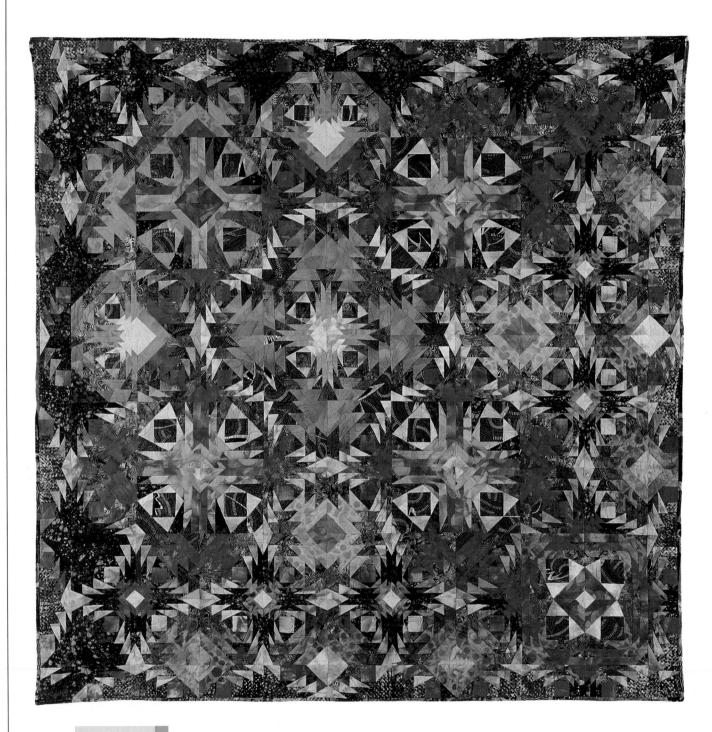

QUASARS

61" x 61", 1994

Cottons, including dyed & air brushed, many by
Debra Lunn, rayon & monofilament threads
Machine pieced on foundation blocks, machine quilted

Laura Murray

MINNEAPOLIS, MINNESOTA

MY QUILTMAKING

Though I have a long history of needlework, I have never been attracted to traditional quiltmaking. But in 1989, to make my daughter the bed quilt she wanted, I took a class. Soon after, I visited the art building at the 1989 Minnesota State fair where Wendy Richardson's quilt NOT QUITE BLACK AND WHITE was displayed. This first "in the cloth" view of a non-traditional quilt opened my eyes to wondrous possibilities.

I knew I had found my perfect form of creative self-expression. It had never occurred to me that I could create my own designs for my needlework. Once I discovered contemporary quilts, I became completely hooked. Not a day has gone by since my first class that I have not been engaged in some way with quiltmaking.

I am currently working on a pictorial Art Nouveau design, and am learning to produce my own original fabrics in addition to collecting unusual textiles from around the world. I really can't tell you exactly where it is all headed; it's the process of "pushing the edges" of my own development that is important to me.

MY LOG CABIN QUILT

I prefer working directly with fabric color and texture, so I drafted the two basic blocks and then sewed four identical blocks to form a set. The rest of the design grew around that unit. In the past I've used the Log Cabin for family quilts meant to be used on the bed. This is the first time I've used it for an art quilt, a quilt which requires more attention to detail and design, and is meant to hang on the wall.

QUASARS involves more discipline and structure than my work usually does. Several days after I began the design, my daughter's neck was fractured in a swimming pool accident. She is now completely recovered, but for three months there were many unknowns. I found the process of working with small pieces, one unit at a time, and then juxtapositioning them with other pieces very soothing. I lacked the energy to be spontaneous; all I could handle was one piece at a time, building as I went. When my life is "in order," my work is much more free-flowing and spontaneous. I usually have little interest in the structure or repetition of traditional geometric design.

The Log Cabin design has always been a favorite because it lends itself to the use of numerous fabrics. Never having made the Pineapple version, I was intrigued by an off-center version in a magazine.

See page 103 for patterns.

17

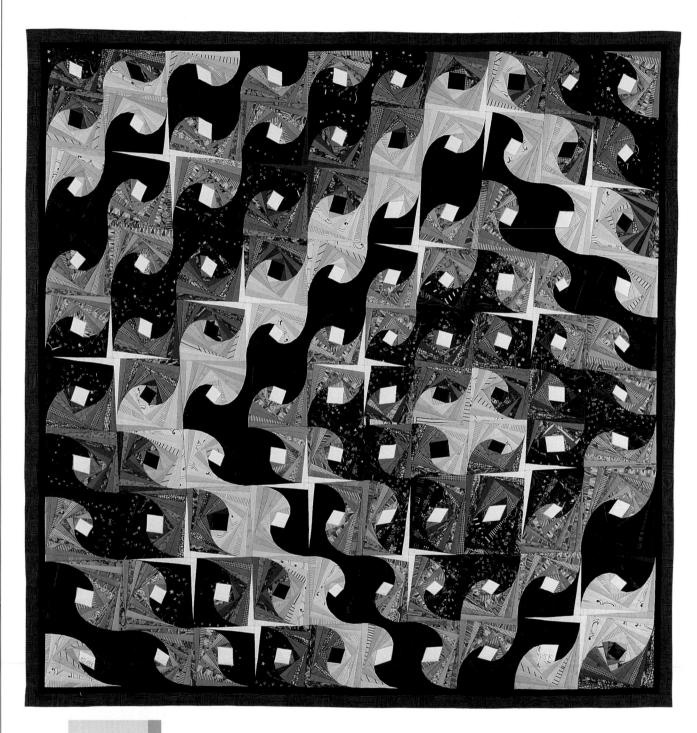

SUPERNOVA 1994

50" x 50", 1994

Cottons

Machine pieced & quilted

Barbara T. Kaempfer

METTMENSTETTEN, SWITZERLAND

MY QUILTMAKING

I began quilting in 1982, just after I moved with my family from Switzerland to Raleigh, North Carolina, where my husband had been transferred for three years. At first it was quite difficult to adjust in a completely new environment. Luckily, there was another Swiss family in Raleigh. The first time we visited their home, Sonja, the wife, showed me the antique quilts she was collecting. Never having paid attention to quilts, I could not understand her excitement. I thought these quilts were pretty, but that was it.

In September Sonja asked me to attend a quilt class with her. Having always loved to sew and having made most of my clothing, I agreed. Quilting changed my life. I "caught the virus."

Quilting has become very important in my life: I'm happy when working on a quilt. A wonderful side effect has been the many wonderful people I have met through quilting.

In addition to making quilts, my book *Log Cabin with a Twist.* is being published and I am teaching new classes – there are many projects I would like to complete!

MY LOG CABIN QUILT

When I begin a new quilt, I never know exactly how it will turn out. The risk of a new project is fun. I've been working with the curved Log Cabin technique for four years, rotating the shapes to create the illusion of curves. In this quilt I experimented with how this technique looks when applied with a traditional setting like Barn Raising.

Each block needed to be drawn individually because the uneven blocks are all different. The fabric was sewn directly on this paper, by machine, and the quilt was then machine quilted. I started in the center of the Barn Raising, working my way around. By using white fabric on the outer most strip of some of the blocks, stars emerged. My husband came up with the name SUPERNOVA. He thinks the red star amongst the other stars in the night sky shows the explosion of a star which is called Supernova. Often family members or friends are the ones who name my quilts.

There are so many more possibilities for curved Log Cabin quilts that I think I'll work with the pattern for some time to come.

In 1991 I discovered the Curved Log Cabin pattern and was immediately hooked. I never work especially for a contest, but it is great to find out that a quilt you've made might fit the conditions of a competition.

See page 99 for patterns.

UNDER THE LOG CABIN SKY

53" x 50", 1994

Hand-dyed cottons, rayon & monofilament threads

Free-form patchwork, hand appliqué &

machine quilting

Ann Fahl

RACINE, WISCONSIN

MY QUILTMAKING

I took my first quilting class in 1978, and completed my first sampler quilt that same year. Over time, I've become a full-time quilt artist and now devote my time to making art quilts, teaching, lecturing, and writing. Awards won along the way keep me working on new projects. And perhaps even more importantly, my husband continues to be supportive of my work and my achievements.

I never stop quilting – sometimes I take a break, but my next quilt is always the most challenging and exciting.

MY LOG CABIN QUILT

This quilt is the fourth in a series of garden quilts based on my free-form patchwork technique. When I learned of the "New Quilts from Old Favorites" Log Cabin contest, exhibit, and book, I had three quilts already finished. Two used Log Cabin roses, but the quilts were all too small to qualify, so I designed this piece using a similar garden, and added a goldfish pond.

I have always been fascinated by the many variations possible with the Log Cabin design. I had never experimented with the pattern because I felt it was too traditional. In 1993 my first garden quilt needed flowers – and an irregular Log Cabin block in red and rose with a gold center made a perfect rose. I used a similar rose garden for this quilt. The sky and goldfish are also Log Cabin blocks, with variations forming the fins and tail.

The rose garden section went quickly, but piecing the 36 blocks for the sky took every ounce of stamina I had. It was very tedious. Next came the goldfish pond. The hand-dyed water fabric was cut and seemed a peaceful addition the quilt. The fish proved to be quite a problem.

A half dozen fish and two months later, I finally created the fish I'd imagined and began machine quilting the piece. At one point I boldly put a spool of variegated orange thread on my machine, and started adding the eyes, mouth, scales, and fins. The quilt finally worked! I knew at last that the quilt was a success, and I declared peace with the fish in the pond.

The minute I learned of this contest, I envisioned the quilt I wanted to make. I am pleased with this finished piece, which looks very much like my original mental picture. This rarely happens.

See page 62 for a piecing technique and a pattern.

21

ELVIS AND THE PENGUINS

53" x 53", 1994

Hand-dyed cottons

Hand appliquéd, machine pieced & hand quilted

Nancy S. Brown

OAKLAND, CALIFORNIA

MY QUILTMAKING

My mother taught me to quilt after she took a class in 1982. I enjoyed painting with watercolors and thought that quiltmaking might be like painting with fabric. My first quilt, a penguin quilt, took several years to complete, but since then I have been hooked on quilting. I make mostly animal themed appliqué quilts, but this quilt is mostly pieced. People might be surprised that I don't use a hoop, frame, or thimble. I could never get the hang of them and found that I could do just as well without them. You don't necessarily have to do things the way that everyone else does.

I continue to make quilts because I really enjoy making them. I love the fabric, I love the designing, and I love the process of putting it all together. Quiltmaking is a wonderful creative outlet for me. I think that as long as I live I will continue to make animal quilts. I think that animals are wonderful, important parts of this world and deserve to be celebrated and preserved. Their inspiration for design possibilities is endless and I can't imagine ever growing tired of animals or quiltmaking.

MY LOG CABIN QUILT

This quilt started because I wanted to try a portrait using appliqué only. I have always used fabric paint to create faces. I wanted to make a recognizable face, and Elvis seemed a good choice. I thought that outer triangles filled in with a Log Cabin type design might make a striking frame. A penguin fanatic, I naturally thought the quilt also needed some penguins.

A story goes along with this quilt: It is a little known fact that before Elvis became famous he toured the country with a highly talented group of penguins. Petty jealousies and squabbles over the nightly menu eventually led the band to break up. The penguins went home to Argentina and Elvis... well he became Elvis. Recent rumors have surfaced suggesting that Elvis is indeed alive and living in Argentina with his old friends. The penguins have no comment.

I am pleased that this quilt makes people laugh. I had a lot of fun making it.

Working with the Log Cabin pattern, I have grown to like its simple yet very striking design.

Most people who know me know that I'm a quiltmaker, but very few people know that I am an Elvis fan. I am also a penguin fanatic.

See page 70 for tips.

EYE OF THE STORM

78" x 92", 1994

Cottons

Machine pieced & hand quilted

Deanna D. Dison

SPEARSVILLE, LOUISIANA

MY QUILTMAKING

I learned to quilt in the 1950's as a teenager. My mother made quilts so I was able to see the construction process. After marrying in 1960 and starting a family, I began to make easy traditional quilts for use. Then in 1986 I really got serious about quiltmaking. That year I made 10 quilts to give as Christmas gifts. For the next four years I made traditional quilts and began to enter them in local fairs and shows. I never won prizes, so I decided to take classes and see what I was doing wrong. I learned to use a rotary cutter, and discovered many other tips and short cuts.

Since 1990 I have made only original designs, except for quilts made in a few workshops. I continue making quilts because I just love doing it. I always have so many ideas in my mind that I would like to incorporate in my designs. I not only want my designs to be pleasing to look at, but I also want them to evoke a feeling. I want them to show depth and movement. I like to take the traditional and use it in a new way to accomplish that.

MY LOG CABIN QUILT

This quilt was not made to be a beautiful, soothing, easy-to-look-at quilt. Rather, it was meant to convey the unsettling feeling experienced in times of disaster, whether it be a flood, earthquake, hurricane, fire, or the loss of a dear loved one. At such times we experience a feeling of helplessness; we recognize we can do nothing to change the events.

This quilt was made about six months after the death of my granddaughter, so such feelings were on my mind. I had worked with the Log Cabin design before, but in a traditional way. This time I wanted to use it in an original way with the swirl block I had drawn earlier. It took me a couple of months just to design the quilt. I drew the design several times, and then had to experiment with colors. I started off with browns, then I went to gray-blues, purples, and oranges. But the oranges didn't work in fabric, so I finally put reds in place of the oranges and they worked great. Once I got it on paper and the fabrics chosen everything went together easily. I enjoy using the traditional in a new way.

The contest is what most inspired my choice of pattern, but I had already drawn the black and gray swirl block. I wanted to use it some way, and I decided this would be the time.

See page 89 for patterns.

THE GIRLS AT HOME

70" x 54", 1993

Cottons, linen; cotton, rayon & metallic
threads & wool yarn; hand painted background
Machine appliquéd, machine pieced,
free-motion machine quilting & embellishment

Michele M. Duell

SPRINGFIELD, VIRGINIA

MY QUILTMAKING

I began making quilts in 1984, after a fellow graduate student showed me a quilt she was working on, gave me an instruction book, and took me to a quilt store. I was immediately fascinated. The person most responsible for my being a quiltmaker is my mother, Ruth Duell. I have heard the "snick-snick" of dressmaking shears since before I was born. I began to sew in high school, so when I finally discovered quiltmaking, the technical part was second nature.

My maternal grandmother, Agnes Callihan, made quilts until her death in 1936, but I was not aware of this until 1994. I am making quilts, rather than working in another media, largely because I want to honor the traditions of my foremothers. Quiltmaking is a political act to me. Long before I knew of my grandmother's involvement, I was fascinated by quiltmakers of previous generations.

I make art quilts, lead workshops, and sell hand-dyed fabrics to fabric stores and at local quilt shows. I am now working on a series of quilts about historical events in my hometown, Johnstown, Pennsylvania.

MY LOG CABIN QUILT

The mud cloth from which three of the chickens were cut was one of the inspirations for this quilt. I began collecting other chicken and bird fabrics, knowing that I wanted to combine chickens or birds and Log Cabin blocks. I'd made a series of Log Cabin quilts over the past several months.

The second inspiration was a nest. In its component parts, a nest is just sticks and mud, but it's a perfectly suitable place for raising a bird family. I wanted to create a place that was messy but charming. These two inspirations came together and the idea of a chicken coop was born.

THE GIRLS AT HOME is a reaction to our culture's idea that bigger and fancier is better. Chicken coops are often cobbled together from the material at hand. The chickens don't know that they aren't living someplace lavish.

The blocks were individually constructed from strips of fabric and sewn by machine. Most are traditional Log Cabin blocks, including Courthouse Steps and Chimneys and Cornerstones variations.

I showed absolutely no artistic talent in school, and concentrated on music. In college, my best friend was an art major. I was always slightly jealous, wishing that instead of practicing the piano, I could spend my afternoons drawing and painting.

See page 72 for a construction technique.

SKYLIGHTS

63" x 74", 1992

Cottons, monofilament thread

Hand-dyed, machine pieced &

machine quilted

Caryl Bryer Fallert

OSWEGO, ILLINOIS

MY QUILTMAKING

For as long as I can remember, I have expressed myself through artwork. My formal training was primarily in design, drawing, and studio painting, and my mother taught me to sew and crochet. I can remember making a dress for myself when I was about 10. By the time I was in my twenties I had taught myself to knit, embroider, and sew curtains and slipcovers as well as clothing. I learned cutting and fitting skills in the 1970's by teaching myself to build furniture and make stained glass.

In 1974, my husband and I bought an old farm in Missouri from Ida Vohs, a 79-year-old woman who had made quilts her whole life, traditional designs put together with a remarkable instinct for color and composition.

In 1976, I ordered a book on quilting and made my first quilt, with ⅝" seams. By 1983, I had given up painting, stained glass, knitting, and dabbling, and began focusing on fabric as a medium for expression. I now make my living as a professional quilt artist. Quilting consumes all of my time and all of my energy, and I love every minute of it.

MY LOG CABIN QUILT

The most important question I ever ask myself is "What would happen if I...?" Fortunately for me, my sense of curiosity has always been stronger than my fear of failure. One day I said, "What would happen if I drew diagonal lines across a big piece of paper, side to side, and top to bottom, and pieced the shapes formed by the lines, like a Log Cabin quilt?" I just had to see, so I did it, and this quilt was the result.

Most of my personal experience with Log Cabin piecing has been in my series called "Refraction," in which Log Cabin piecing is done around a hexagon.

SKYLIGHTS is a scrap quilt made from strips of fabric left over from several of my other quilting projects. Instead of squares or rectangles, I have used quadrilaterals in which no two sides are the same length. The center of each is a deep turquoise, the color of the sky on a cloudless day. This suggested the title SKYLIGHTS.

Once the quilt was completed, my mind began to imagine dozens of variations on this theme. I would like to try all of them.

My favorite traditional quilt block is the Log Cabin. I love the endless interactions that take place between the blocks, and the complex visual texture created by the hundreds of different scrap fabrics used in many of the nineteenth century Log Cabin quilts.

See page 66 for a construction tip.

EXUBERANCE

62" x 82", 1994

Cottons, a few hand-dyed by

Melody Johnson, rayon thread

Machine pieced & quilted

FINALIST

Wanda S. Hanson

SANDWICH, ILLINOIS

MY QUILTMAKING

I began quilting in 1957 when as a junior in high school I made a baby quilt for a cousin. No one else in my family sewed, so everything I made got rave reviews. I have made several hundred, all by machine except two. Experimenting with many styles and techniques, I have come to original-design quilts as my favorites. These quilts are combinations of ideas collected and tried through the years.

I think the thing that surprises people most about my quilts is the variety of fabrics I work with. I make a lot of wild, bright quilts with the wonderful fabrics available today; but I also like to make subdued plaid quilts and soft flowered print quilts.

I have always loved touching fabric and playing with colors, and quiltmaking includes both. To have a finished project to show what I have done with my time is also important to me; self-satisfaction with what I am doing with my life keeps me focused. The sharing of my talent through teaching quiltmaking and the giving of quilts as gifts is very fulfilling.

MY LOG CABIN QUILT

Log Cabin has always been one of my favorite blocks. When I started making Crazy Log Cabins, I was doing it to use up my scraps. I never let myself take the technique very seriously. Then one day I realized how happy I was when working on the blocks and how much satisfaction I felt every time I saw them. I finally let myself consider them a legitimate part of my quilting activity. As I made more and more blocks, I decided to make a big quilt – it would be a gift to myself.

I have made 17 Log Cabin quilts. I have made many traditional style quilts over the years and have taught others how to make them. I love seeing people enjoy the freedom of expression that quiltmaking allows.

I am most pleased with the joyful, colorful appearance of this quilt. There isn't anything I would change about it if I began again. When people look at this quilt, I would like them to feel the same joy and freedom that I felt while making it.

The Log Cabin pattern is one that both beginners and experienced quilters can enjoy. I will continue to make Log Cabin quilts, trying as many of the variations as possible.

See page 80 for a construction pattern.

JUST BECAUSE

58" x 58", 1994

Cottons, some hand-dyed by maker & others,

wool batting; cotton blend yarn

Machine pieced, quilted & couched

Barbara Oliver Hartman

FLOWER MOUND, TEXAS

MY QUILTMAKING

I began quiltmaking in about 1980. I taught myself and did not know what I was doing. I also had a full-time job, children at home, and a limited amount of time. It was 1985 before it became a real obsession. By that time, I had found the Quilter's Guild of Dallas and had a circle of "quilt" friends.

Probably what really got me "hooked" was entering a quilt in a show. I remember how I felt when I saw people viewing and making comments about something I made. It was quite intoxicating.

Three people have been very surprised by my quiltmaking – my mother, my husband, and myself. My mother still shakes her head and says, "I could never get you to sew." Owner of a small dressmaking company, she tried. It was a real test of wills.

In 1989, I began a pattern company which grows each year, I make quilts that I want to make, I have the support of a great husband, mom, sister, children, and friends. What else could a person ask for.

MY LOG CABIN QUILT

JUST BECAUSE was made for this contest. I rarely participated in "challenge" projects but find that whenever I do, participation pushes me to explore areas that I normally would not. The fabrics were chosen and the blocks begun before the overall plan was finalized.

I had always used the Log Cabin pattern in a very traditional way, usually in clothing. I have always been interested in the various ways this pattern has been used. I knew that in my quilt I wanted the blocks to be made in the standard Log Cabin way, but using fabrics that would keep the quilt from looking traditional.

I also wanted to set it differently and decided to use a square-in-a-square format. The use of a background fabric in the corners gave the quilt a medallion effect. The yarn, which was sewn on last with the feed dogs down and the machine set on a zigzag stitch, was used as a surface design tool to soften the geometric pattern of the overall quilt.

Over the years quiltmaking has really given my life a joy and fulfillment that I never expected.

It was fun to see this quilt develop, change several times, and evolve into a finished piece with secondary patterns. Log Cabin is a great pattern to work with because the design can be bold or soft and offers endless possibilities.

See page 68 for a design tip.

SPELLBOUND

81" x 81", 1993

Cottons; some overdyed

Machine pieced on tear-away foundation,

hand quilted

Allison Lockwood

SHELL BEACH, CALIFORNIA

MY QUILTMAKING

I began quilting in 1986 after the birth of my second daughter. My former passion was ballet. As it became increasingly difficult to leave my young family to attend classes, I realized I had to give it up. To ease my disappointment, I signed up for a beginning patchwork class. I've traded one passion for another.

Currently, I make mostly large wall quilts that use a traditional block in an innovative way. I love to hand quilt and like to make quilting an important part of the design. My newest quilt mixes new fabrics, antique fabrics, and fabrics salvaged from thrift store clothing.

I have three young daughters, so much of my quilting is done during the "guilt free" hours they're asleep. I have surprised myself in that I spend so many hours hand quilting. I find it to be very hypnotic.

My mother, June Alexis, is partially responsible for my becoming a quiltmaker. I was brought up by a mother who was and still is in a constant state of creative frenzy. She always encouraged artistic expression so I can't imagine a life without some form of creative endeavor.

MY LOG CABIN QUILT

I've spent many hours spellbound by the quilts in my large collection of books. I've especially been attracted to nineteenth century Pineapple Log Cabins. SPELLBOUND is an original design variation using the traditional Pineapple Log Cabin block which has a very complex appearance. To learn how to piece one, I took a one-day class from Dixie Haywood. I started this quilt about a year later.

I made another Log Cabin quilt I call LAVISH MACTAVISH specifically to enter in the contest. After working on this quilt for over a year, I realized the quilt would not be finished in time for the entry deadline. Two weeks before the deadline it dawned on me that SPELLBOUND might qualify. I'm glad I entered it!

The quilt is made from 81 identically constructed blocks. I'd like to experiment with designing other simple blocks. I don't feel very directed toward complicated piecing. I'm convinced that sometimes the simplest piecing can make the most fascinating quilts – if the fabric choices are exciting.

I've made a couple of Log Cabin quilts – it's my favorite pattern. I could spend the rest of my quilting days doing nothing but Log Cabin designs and never lose my enthusiasm.

See page 82 for a pattern.

FOUR AND TWENTY BLACKBIRDS
DIVIDED BY TWO

72" x 84", 1994

Cottons

Machine pieced, hand appliquéd & hand quilted

Catherine McIntee

TROY, MICHIGAN

MY QUILTMAKING

I first pieced fabric squares together as a seventh grader in 1965. I made my first real quilt in 1973, and haven't stopped since. Quilting occupies my mind during much of my waking hours, and occupies my hands as much as I can possibly fit it in.

My lifestyle may be a little unusual for a quilter in several ways. By profession, I am a banker. As a Senior Vice President of a 12 billion dollar midwest financial institution, my job consumes much of my life. I also have three terrific children, ages 14, 11, and 5. My husband is the full-time caregiver for our children. Both quilting and my husband Barry are responsible for my sanity.

I continue to quilt because I must. It is as much a part of my life as getting up, going to work, and coming home. I am constantly hand quilting antique tops, always have a design idea going, am machine piecing something, and have an appliqué project in the works. Quilting is my therapy, my artistic outlet, and satisfies my very real need to produce something that has a lasting value.

MY LOG CABIN QUILT

The inspiration for this quilt started with the border fabric, on which all other fabric and color choices were based. The design inspiration, on the other hand, was a combination of two influences. The Log Cabin design with a Sawtooth border was spotted in an antique Ohio quilt, and the center appliqué block is taken from Jeanna Kimball's book *Red and Green: An Appliqué Tradition*. I modified the central block, replacing the birds with ones I liked better. I then designed a larger single bird on a berry stem to fill in the setting blocks, and a lone stem with berries for the setting triangles.

When I was first laying out the design I thought that I would put two blackbirds in the center block, 10 in the setting blocks, and 12 in the setting triangles – hence 24 blackbirds. The popular child's nursery rhyme immediately came to mind. Later I had to eliminate the birds in the small setting triangles. I had had the title in my head for a few weeks, but was now down to only 12 birds – hence the title: FOUR AND TWENTY BLACKBIRDS DIVIDED BY TWO.

The very first quilt I made was a Courthouse Steps pattern – a variation of the Log Cabin block. I have also hand quilted an antique Log Cabin top, and I am currently working on a miniature Log Cabin quilt that's going to be a beauty!

See page 105 for selected patterns.

BUTTERFLIES ARE FREE

77" x 88", 1994

Yukata, fabrics from kimonos, Sashiko thread

Machine pieced, hand appliquéd & hand quilted

Lois Monieson

KINGSTON, ONTARIO

MY QUILTMAKING

In 1985 I took a quilting course at a summer program and loved it. One of my first quilting teachers was Doris Waddell, who has been a winner twice in AQS shows. Another early teacher of mine was Patricia Morris, who inspired me to excellence.

An aunt of mine who lived on a farm was a quilter. I always told her I wanted to quilt, but never got around to doing it while she was alive. I hope she knows how much I enjoy quilting now.

I love to go to big quilt shows and conferences and take as many workshops as I can. The continuing stimulation of attending these events and entering competitions where my quilts are shown makes me want to make more quilts. I also buy many quilt, art, and design books and quilt magazines.

I plan to keep attending workshops and conferences, entering competitions, and buying books for as long as I can. This cross-country stimulation and the many friends I make through participation replace the by-gone days of the quilting bee for me.

MY LOG CABIN QUILT

I have always liked the Log Cabin design and had already made two Log Cabin quilts, but this quilt was inspired by Kuroha Shizuko's Clamshell design shown in her book. The quilt uses uneven logs that result in a five-and-a-half inch finished block. In her quilt Kuroha Shizuko stacked them on top of each other, but I interlocked them as Moneca Calvert does in some of her Clamshell quilts.

This quilt is made from Japanese Yukata fabric I purchased during two trips to Japan and in Berkeley, California. The border and some of the other fabrics in the center were cut from used kimonos. The butterflies were cut from an antique kimono as well. I am pleased with the quilt, but wish I could have had a few more fabric choices for some of the Clamshells.

Since making BUTTERFLIES ARE FREE, I have made another uneven Log Cabin design. In these quilts I have stretched the Log Cabin design to encompass a culture other than my own, using Japanese fabrics and elements of Japanese design. I am pleased that this quilt tells my story.

When visiting Japan in 1992, I purchased a book of Log Cabin designs by Kuroha Shizuko. I was flabbergasted! They were Log Cabin designs, but they didn't look the least bit like any I'd seen before.

See page 76 for patterns.

GEESE IN THE BARN

85" x 85", 1994

Cottons & cotton blends

Machine pieced & hand quilted

Charlotte Roach

STRATFORD, CONNECTICUT

MY QUILTMAKING

I became involved in quiltmaking in 1964 as a young mother. I had been sewing since a teen, so I was facing the dilemma of an accumulation of scraps. I asked my mother what other homemakers did with them and she gave me a 16-page pamphlet entitled *Patchwork Quilts* (1940). I loved the cover quilt and set about to make it. Not much information was given beyond a pencil drawing of the set and the dimensions for the hexagon pattern piece. I eventually made this quilt, as well as quilts for each of my children's beds.

By 1971 I had stopped quilting. In September 1981 I enrolled in a sampler quilt class and made a quilt that has won several awards. I enjoyed quilting for five more years before laying it aside again for eight years. Now I am on my third cycle of quiltmaking and am not only engulfed in scraps, but have also become a fabricaholic who purchases fabric for "potential creations."

I have many other hobbies, but it seems far wiser for me to invest my time in creating a quilt that could bring others joy for generations to come.

MY LOG CABIN QUILT

Unaware of the contest until after my quilt had been completed, I was inspired to make this quilt by a visit to my daughter and her family in Minnesota. On their farm we toured a rustic old barn with birds flying in and out, through the hayloft. Wanting to use at least two traditional patterns and pare down my scrap collection, I started with the center four Log Cabin squares and the sashing of geese weaving in and out. I liked the way it looked and decided to expand it to comforter size for our master bedroom.

In the past it has taken me about one and a half years per large quilt. This summer I decided to try a different approach. I committed a least one hour a day to working on this quilt. I kept a log of my time and found myself competing with my previous time on each block. Most days I enjoyed three or four hours of time on my project, and was able to keep up my pace and my interest for the duration. My quilt was completed in only two months, from start to finish, 140 hours. There are 1,865 pieces, many individually cut, and all placed in such a way as to avoid proximity to a similar print.

The longer I quilt, the more I appreciate the subtle complexity of the Log Cabin design. I realize that I have only skimmed the surface of experimenting with this pattern. I'm sure I will use it again and again.

See page 73 for patterns.

41

RAISING A "NEW AGE" BARN

72" x 60", 1994

Cottons & cotton blends

Machine pieced, machine quilted &

hand beaded

Cynthia Smith

ST. AUGUSTINE, FLORIDA

MY QUILTMAKING

In the late 1980's I began attending college as an adult. The plan was to become a school guidance counselor, but an art appreciation elective changed my focus to interior design.

In fall 1990, I became good friends with a fellow adult student, Michael Gilroy, who had AIDS. His illness soon made college impossible; however, our friendship continued. Michael encouraged me, giving me permission to think of myself as an artist. That fall, research exposed me to the book *The Quilt – Stories From the Names Project*. This book had little to do with technique and everything to do with personal expression. I decided to try just one quilt over our Christmas break. Anyone can probably guess the rest. The aforementioned project became a large painting based on traditional quilt blocks, a painting about my friend Michael.

When Michael died, I made his panel for the Names Project based on my painting. Quiltmaking has given me a voice for which I am truly grateful.

MY LOG CABIN QUILT

The basic layout for this quilt was inspired by curiosity about how curved and straight Log Cabin blocks would interact. This question was easily answered with the help of the computer software "ElectricQuilt®," which made it possible to draw only two blocks and set up an entire layout.

This design was one that wouldn't go away! I had attempted this quilt once before, using white and red palm tree fabric for the centers and having traditional fabrics on the left side and more contemporary fabrics on the right. Unable to finish more than half of the blocks because of personal problems, I put the entire project on hold for almost a year. Those blocks have since been re-cycled in a story quilt. When the call came out for this contest, I re-examined my line drawing, selected new fabrics, and approached the design in a more painterly fashion.

I am most pleased with the decision to add the borders and have the barn "explode" into the borders. This is a barn with a conforming side, and also a rebellious side which could not be contained by tradition.

Often the fabrics I purchase can only be taken in small doses, such as in the narrow pieces of a Log Cabin block. My sketchbook is full of designs I would like to try in Log Cabin blocks.

See page 61 for tips on adding beading to quilts.

LOG CABIN SQUARED

75" x 75", 1994

Cottons

Machine pieced on paper foundation blocks &

machine quilted by Fran McEachem

Nancy Taylor

PLEASANTON, CALIFORNIA

MY QUILTMAKING

I made my first quilt in 1975, for my then five-year-old daughter's bed. I would have to say that my mother, Margaret Vantine, had some responsibility for my becoming a quilter since we became quilters together through the making of this quilt. Neither one of us had ever made a quilt, but she offered to quilt it if I pieced and appliquéd it, so we learned together.

Today, my mother still quilts some of my quilts with the tiniest, most beautiful stitches. My oldest daughter, for whom the quilt was made, has since learned to quilt and produce tiny, even stitches too. This skill has skipped a generation; I remain in awe of both of them.

In addition to making quilts, for eight years I was co-owner of Going to Pieces, a quilt shop in Pleasanton, California.

I have recently been creating my own fabric designs for my quilts, using fabric dyes. I spray, paint, immersion dye, and use wax resist to create patterning. I enjoy this aspect and will be concentrating my energies on producing quilts that are completely my own expression.

MY LOG CABIN QUILT

This quilt was inspired by a black and white photograph of an antique quilt with blocks set on point. This set offered strong graphic possibilities for a contemporary version of a very traditional pattern.

I have made two other Log Cabin quilts, each time motivated by the desire to create something different with this rather chunky design unit. This time I decided to let the entire quilt echo the individual block design of concentric squares. I will probably be drawn to the Log Cabin again by the challenge it presents.

This quilt was made with and for the joy of working with color. I liked modulating and adjusting each color within its own band, and working with prints that added "visual texture," an element second only in importance to color.

I was pleased with the resulting integration of strong graphic design and color. This quilt hangs on my living room wall, and I am energized when I walk in and feel its radiating color.

The Log Cabin block is one of the oldest pieced block patterns and one of the most beloved. It is also, as a design unit, one of the most chunky and rigid, with its repeating concentric squares. So, of course, it presents a challenge!

See page 86 for a pattern.

CABIN IN THE WILLOWS

72" x 72", 1994

Cottons

Machine pieced & hand quilted

Diane Turscak

SAFETY HABOR, FLORIDA

MY QUILTMAKING

I began quilting officially in 1975 at a six-week class at the YMCA. But I've always loved quilts and actually made one at age 10. The next quilt was made in 1970 for my son's birth and was a Four-Patch made with the scraps of my maternity clothes. I then began making baby quilts for friends. The greatest compliment to me is when recipients love my quilts so much that they are in tatters by the time their owners are three or four.

Everyone knows I'm addicted to quiltmaking and fabric. I even dress like a quilter, in patchwork jeans and shirts. I even have a Century 21 gold jacket that is pieced and incorporates tiny houses. You probably can't tell it, because of my hair, but I'm wearing it in my photo.

Quilting to me is a way of life, as is living in my farmhouse, built in the 1920's. My mother is an artist, and I was always allowed to be as creative as I wanted to be. I later found out she taught me to sew because she hated to!

MY LOG CABIN QUILT

I've always loved Log Cabin quilts and wanted to make one using all the Log Cabin types: Pineapple, Courthouse Steps, the traditional Log Cabin. I spotted a design which incorporated several of these designs. I worked with the central design, small houses, and Pineapple blocks, and added the rest, including willow trees based on drawings in *Branching Out Tree Quilts* by Carolann Palmer. Influenced by the Flip and Sew paper templates Mary B. Golden used to make her quilt WELCOME HOME 1988, I used those techniques.

I've often thought a quilter could easily get hooked on the Log Cabin pattern because of the vast amount of possibilities it offers. I have done quite a few Log Cabins, from miniatures to king-size quilts. I'm sure I'll work with the pattern again and again.

I hope viewers experience a sense of tranquillity when they see this quilt; I hope they feel as though they were on vacation. If they also notice all the different variations, that's great. I subtitled the quilt "Log Cabin x 5."

I get ideas for quilts wherever I go. I feel that if you use a pattern designed by someone else, you have the advantage of their "tribute" and should be able to improve upon it. You should try to make your quilt even better ....

See page 97 for a design diagram.

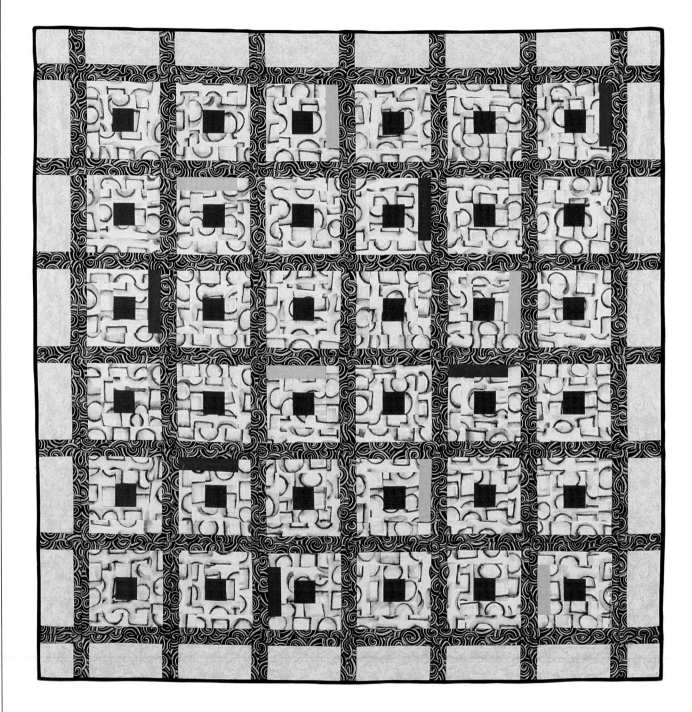

HOMAGE TO MONDRIAAN VII:
A GREEN QUILT

64" x 64", 1991

Cottons, cotton & monofilament threads

Machine pieced & machine quilted

Meiny Vermaas-van der Heide

TEMPE, ARIZONA

MY QUILTMAKING

I clearly remember the picture in *ARIADNE*, the Dutch needle arts magazine that introduced me to quilts – it was an attic bedroom with a Log Cabin quilt in pinks and grays on the bed. So much did I desire to have such a beautiful quilt for my own bed, that I decided to make my first quilt in 1982, the only quilt I ever made in the Netherlands. Although it was pieced and quilted on the sewing machine, it was still three years in the making, mostly because of the lack of suitable filler material and a floor space big enough to stretch the layers.

Upon moving to the USA in 1985, I wanted to learn more about quilts firsthand. Little did I know how quilts could ease foreigners like me into the American social fabric. Here I found quilts to be very interwoven with the country's historical and cultural heritage. I felt kinship with the women immigrants, the westward trekking pioneers who had come before me. Before women had the right to vote, many a quilt was made as a way to speak out. As a foreigner here, I do not have the right to vote, but I can use my talents to voice my concerns through my quilts.

MY LOG CABIN QUILT

This quilt was inspired by Mondriaan paintings from his Pier and Ocean series and by an exhibit of Vincent van Gogh drawings I saw in a Dutch museum in 1990. I suddenly realized why Nancy Crow had had us work in black and white solids, black and white prints, neutral and natural colors, and as a grand finale in full color in her Positive/Negative quilt design workshop.

Especially fascinating to me in the exhibit were the "scribbled" drawings, where the density of the scribbled pencil marks caused value differences and beautiful visual texture at the same time. I could envision what I might do with black and white "scribble" fabric I had bought earlier. In the midst of my "Homage to Mondriaan" series, I began to incorporate the scribbled fabrics.

My quilts are my voice. Many of my quilts are labeled as "GREEN QUILTS," which stands for environmental concern expressed in a positive, open-ended way. The charge in the Bible's book of Genesis for us to be "stewards of the earth" is my inspiration for making "GREEN QUILTS."

What interests me most about the simple, traditional Log Cabin pattern is that through fabrics, one can obscure it within the surface or highlight its horizontal and vertical lines through different fabric choices.

See page 64 for construction tips.

49

Log Cabin Patterns

Included in this section are full templates for the traditional Log Cabin pattern in five different sizes. Select the size most appropriate for your fabrics and project plans and try your own hand at this popular pattern.

LOG CABIN
DESIGN SAMPLES

BARN RAISING

STRAIGHT FURROW

SUNSHINE & SHADOW

ZIGZAG

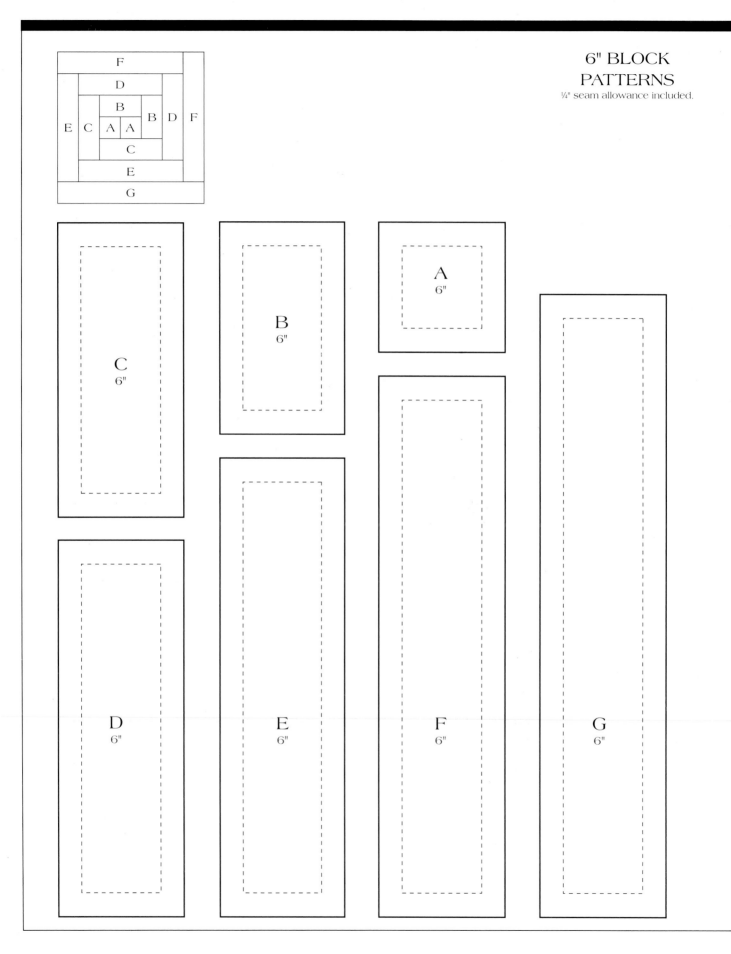

6" BLOCK
PATTERNS
¼" seam allowance included.

F
D
B
E C A A B D F
C
E
G

C
6"

B
6"

A
6"

D
6"

E
6"

F
6"

G
6"

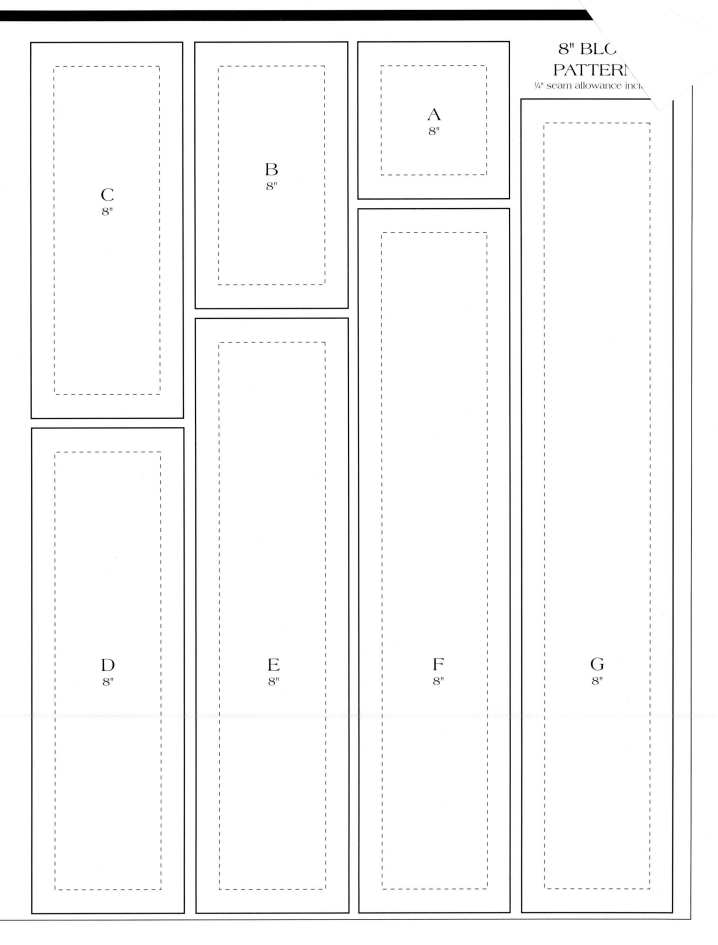

8" BL[OCK]
PATTERN[S]
¼" seam allowance inc[luded]

C
8"

B
8"

A
8"

D
8"

E
8"

F
8"

G
8"

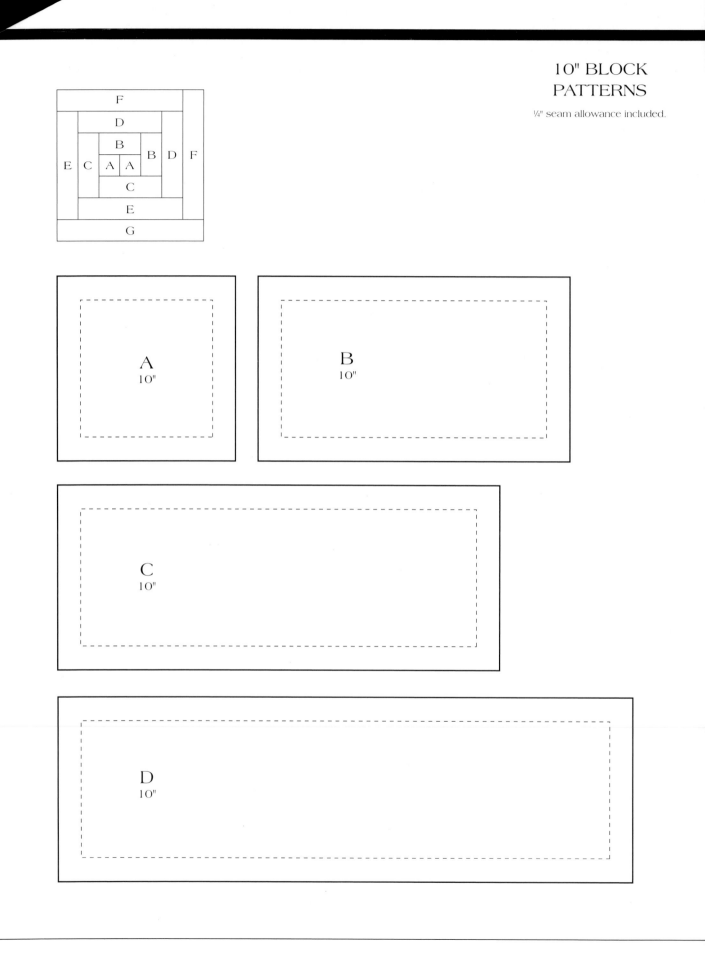

¼" seam allowance included.

A
10"

B
10"

C
10"

D
10"

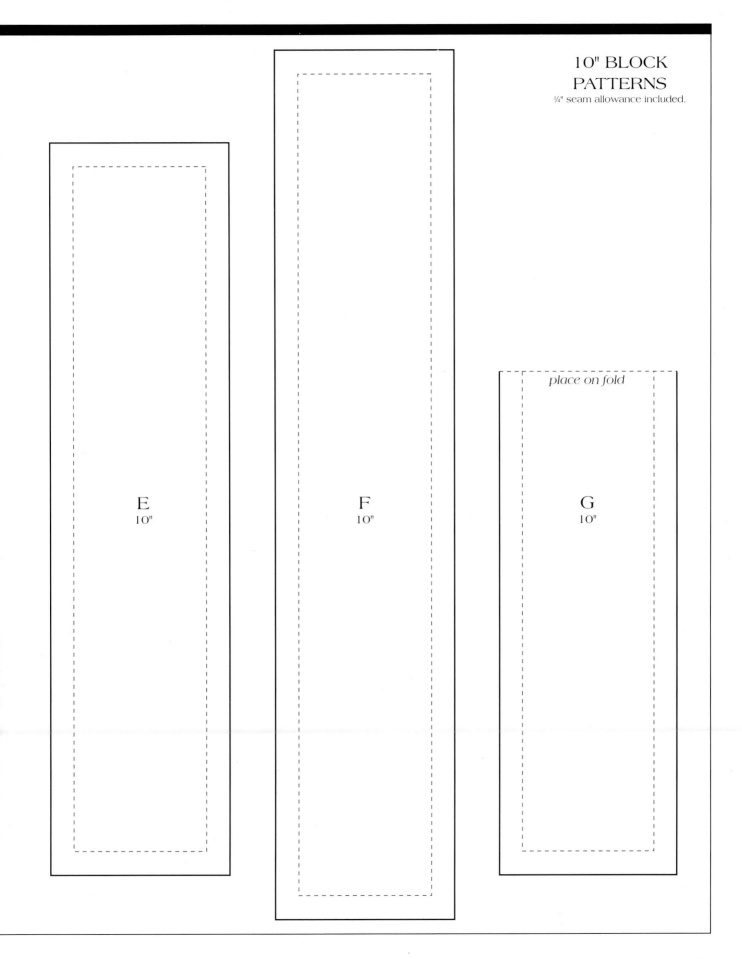

10" BLOCK
PATTERNS
¼" seam allowance included.

E
10"

F
10"

place on fold

G
10"

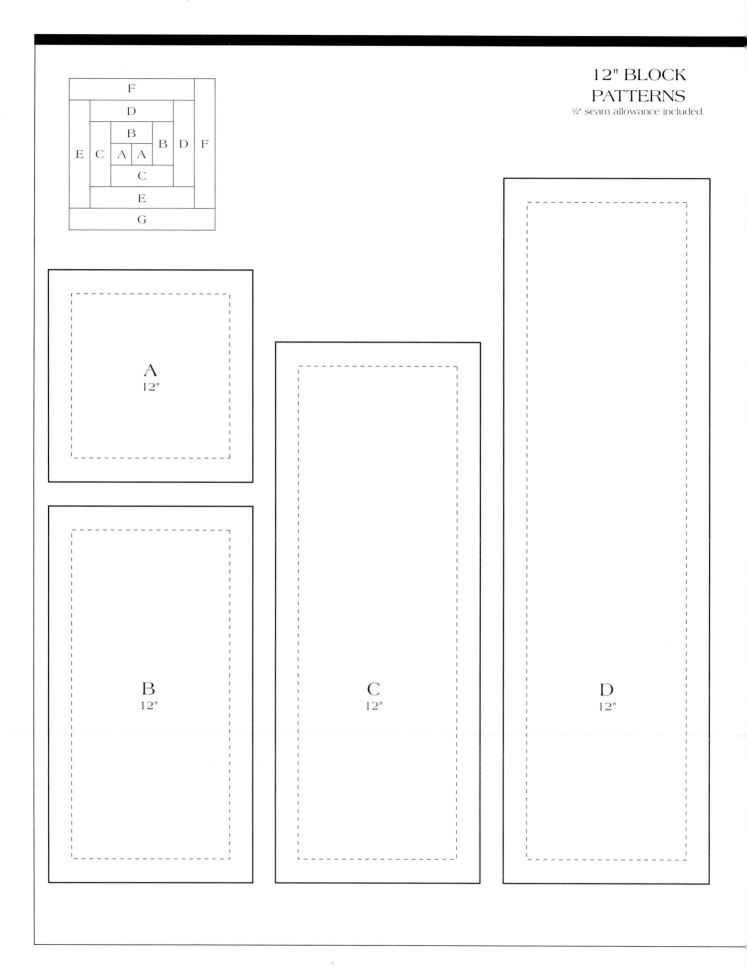

12" BLOCK
PATTERNS
¼" seam allowance included.

F
D
B
E C A A B D F
C
E
G

A
12"

B
12"

C
12"

D
12"

56

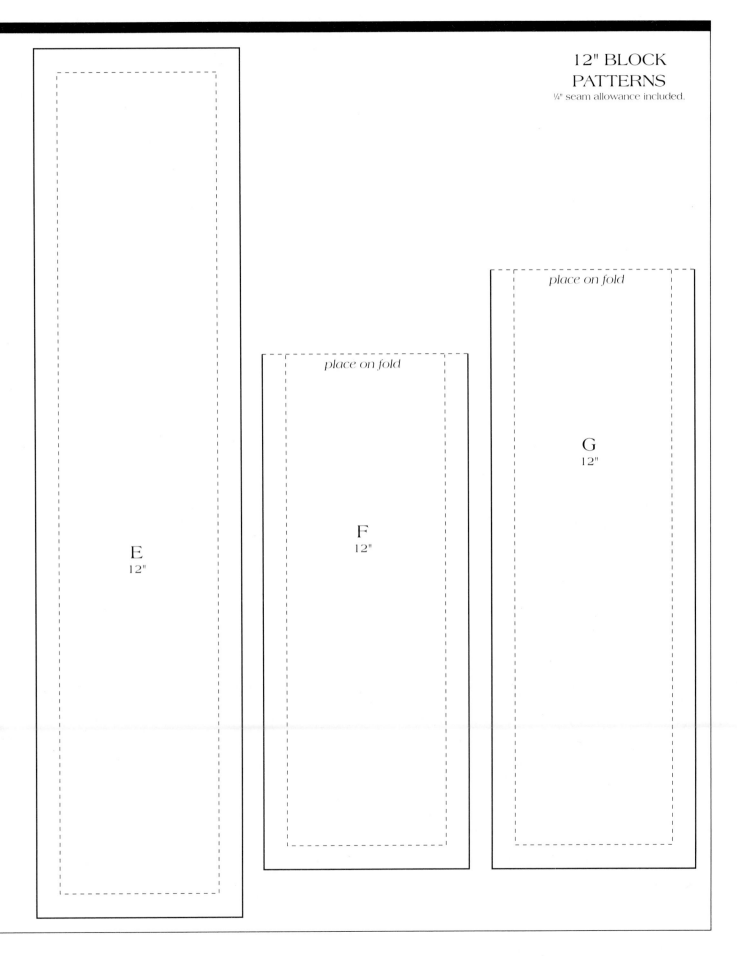

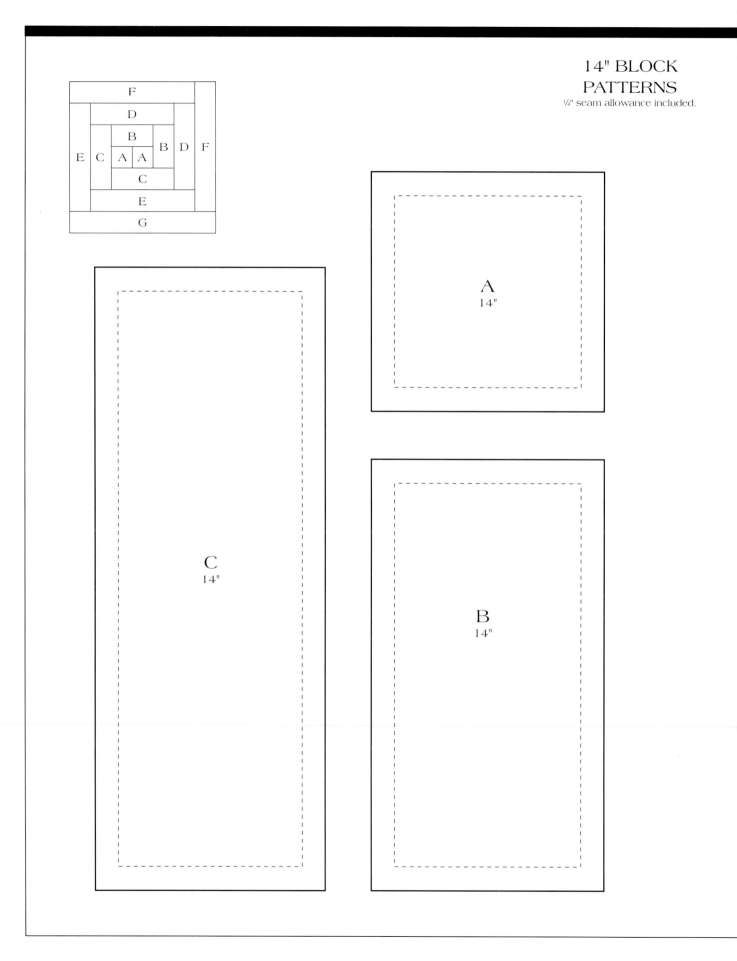

F

D

B

E C A A B D F

C

E

G

A
14"

C
14"

B
14"

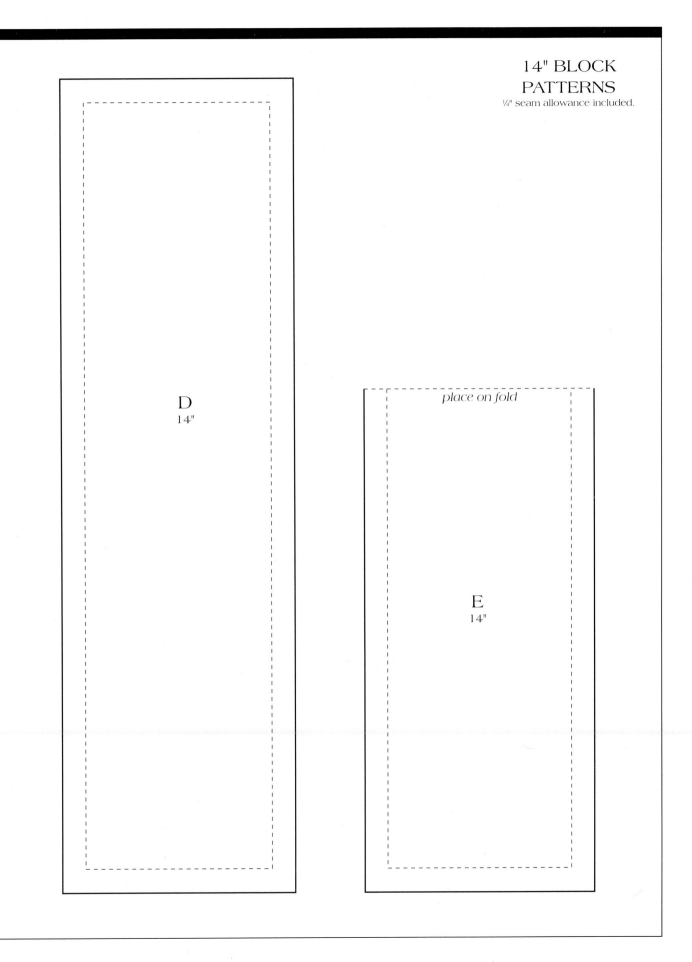

D
14"

place on fold

E
14"

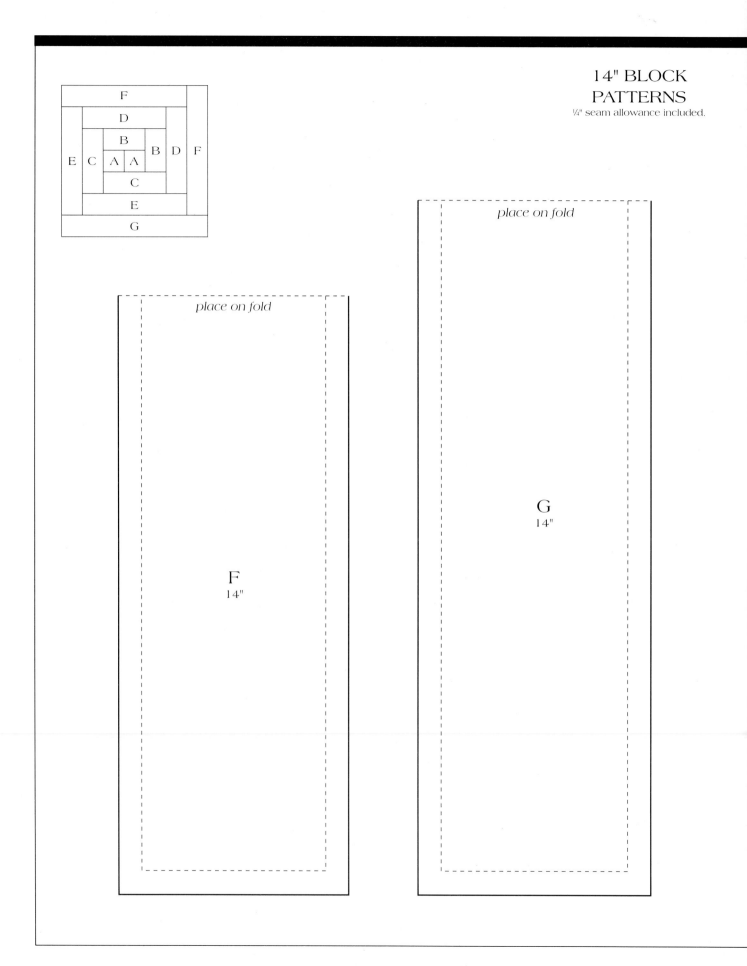

F
D
B
E C A A B D F
C
E
G

place on fold

place on fold

F
14"

G
14"

Working with the Design

TIPS & TECHNIQUES

ADDING BEADING TO QUILTS BY CYNTHIA SMITH

After completing the machine quilting, I felt that I wanted to add emphasis to the areas of my "New Age" barn which I considered to be the "light" halves.

These are a few of the ways I used beading on the quilt:

- Using gold and silver glass rocaille beads and a beading needle, I applied the beads as though they were scattered points of light.

- There were areas of the quilt where I wanted to emphasize the details in the fabric, such as parasols, sea shells, sunflowers and the swirls in the border fabrics. In those areas, I outlined the shapes.

- When folding a beaded quilt for transporting, be sure to cover the surface with an old sheet or large piece of fabric to protect the beads from catching on each other.

This isn't a complicated process, but it allows time for reflection on the piece you have just completed.

RIGHT: *Detail of RAISING A "NEW AGE" BARN featuring some of its beadwork.*

FREE-FORM PATCHWORK:
MAKING A LOG CABIN ROSE
BY ANN FAHL

With the exception of the water in the goldfish pond, UNDER THE LOG CABIN SKY is entirely made using a technique that I call free-form patchwork. Basically, I sew strips onto a lightweight foundation.

Working in this manner, I always start with a small sketch or clear idea, which I translate into a simple, but full-size line drawing on newsprint. Next, I divide up large areas, into small sections; for example; the sky into 36 blocks.

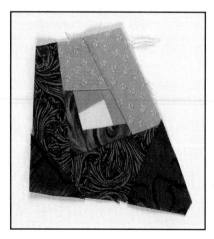

ABOVE: *Log Cabin Rose.*

Instructions for a Log Cabin Rose:

■ Trace the block shape onto ultra-lightweight non-woven interfacing. Cut so the foundation is the finished block size.

■ Cut one-inch strips of fabric, I have found that smaller strips give the illusion of more detail; the drawback is that this necessitates more strips and means it takes more time to fill the block.

■ Place an irregular four sided shape in the center of the flower. This can be varied by using a 3 or 5 sided scrap of fabric. The flower center can be placed anywhere in the block to add variety.

■ Stitch a strip on one side of the center shape. Turn a quarter turn, and stitch another strip, and so on....

■ The strips do not have to be sewn on straight. The next strip can be laid at an angle, so the strip underneath appears to be wide at one end and narrowing to the other.

■ Trim out the excess seam allowance underneath, before pressing, so that other colors don't show or press through. Press after stitching each seam.

■ Sew on strips, until the foundation is covered, with extra hanging over the edges. Then, turn it over and use a ruler and rotary cutter and allow fabric for quarter inch seams and remove the rest. When the finished blocks are pieced together, the foundation fabric isn't included in the seam, so it doesn't add bulk.

■ As in traditional Log Cabin blocks, I designate two sides for the lighter color, and the other two for the dark.

■ Because many of the blocks have odd shapes, sometimes they aren't always appropriate for flowers. If points or corners are too severe, I just add another strip or two, of green or background color made to look like leaves, and this gives the flower a softer look.

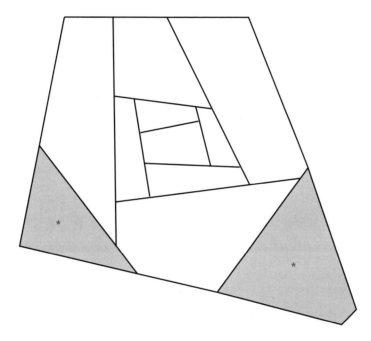

LOG CABIN ROSE
FOUNDATION PATTERN

Shown at 100%.

* = green or background color

ACHIEVING A FLAT,
HEIRLOOM LOOK
BY MEINY VERMAAS-VAN DER HEIDE

Having made many Log Cabin-based quilts, I offer these tips and techniques for creating flat quilt surfaces with an heirloom style look:

PIECING LOG CABIN BLOCKS

- Try not to push or pull the fabric strips. Be patient and let the feed dogs do the work.
- When using a bright center square with lighter strips, zigzag the seam allowances before cutting the bright strip into squares, so fraying of the colored center will not show through the lighter fabric in the finished Log Cabin blocks.
- When pressing Log Cabin blocks, press all seam allowances away from the center square, and let the fabric cool down before adding the next strip or log. Fabric will stretch when slightly wet and hot from the steam. Also, keep in mind that pressing means holding the iron in place for 10 seconds, then lifting the iron to move to the next part to be pressed. Sliding a hot steaming iron over the surface will stretch the fabrics excessively.

PIN BASTING THE QUILT SANDWICH

The way that I "pin baste" my quilt sandwich seems to have a great deal to do with achieving an heirloom look in my quilts. In a 1987 workshop, Harriet Hargrave introduced me to using a batting containing cotton to create machine quilted quilts with an old-fashioned look and touch.

Using batting containing cotton and cotton fabrics, I am able to stretch the layers of the quilt sandwich and "glue" them vertically on a wall, where I can see the whole quilt surface at once and straighten the layers more easily. The vertical lines of paneling in the hallway where I pin baste become guidelines for squaring up the horizontal and vertical lines of the quilt sandwich.

TO PIN BASTE A QUILT

- Stretch the quilt backing (wrong side facing towards you) using 2" masking tape. Put masking tape around the edges, as if you were stretching it in a frame. First put pieces of masking tape at the top edge and each corner. Put more masking tape along the top edge, because it will carry the most weight. During this process it is possible that you need to re-tape certain parts to get the back tautly stretched. Depending on the size of the quilt, the quality of the masking tape, and the humidity in the air; the quilt sandwich will stay up anywhere from three hours to three days.
- "Glue" the batting on top of the quilt backing by gently stroking the batting, and fasten with large quilters pins at the top and sides.
- "Glue" the quilt top over the batting by gently stroking from left to right and top to bottom, following the direction of the seam allowances. Fasten with large quilters pins around the edges of the quilt top, moving the quilters pins from the batting to the quilt top, adding more as needed. During this process keep the horizontal seam lines horizontal, and the vertical seam lines vertical; re-position quilters pins if necessary.
- The quilt sandwich is now ready for "pin basting" with 1" safety pins. I usually place pins 3" to 5" apart, but the spacing you use will depend on the type of batting and how

you plan to machine quilt the sandwich. In "Homage to Mondriaan VII: a GREEN QUILT" I put five safety pins in each block: one in the center square and in each corner of the second round. I prefer to spend more time pinning than to rip out machine quilting because of "false pleats."

■ Pin baste from left to right (when right-handed), putting a horizontal row of safety pins in the middle of the quilt first. Alternate adding a horizontal row of safety pins above and below this middle row.

■ For pin basting the top rows you might want to use a small step ladder, and sitting down on a stool makes pin basting the bottom rows a lot easier.

It is very important that the safety pins go through all layers of the quilt sandwich. To pin baste:

■ insert safety pin through all layers

■ feel how the point of the safety pin touches the wall

■ lift the quilt sandwich just slightly with the safety pin in your right hand and at the same time keep the quilt sandwich down with the pointing and middle finger of your left hand

■ bring the point of the safety pin up again

■ close the safety pin using both hands, your right hand to bring the visible bottom part of the safety pin towards the other

part stuck through the quilt sandwich, and your left pointing finger or middle finger to keep the point of the safety pin up. Older brass safety pins work the best because they are more flexible.

After you have closed the safety pin you should not be able to move it, and on the back of the quilt ¾" of each safety pin should be visible. The drawback of using safety pins is that they can leave small holes in the quilt top, but these disappear when the quilt is laundered, the final step in creating an heirloom look. If a safety pin cuts a thread in one of the fabrics in the quilt top, the tiny hole can be stabilized with Fray-check®.

When the entire center is pin basted, take the quilt down and replace the quilter's pins around the edges with safety pins. I find it easier to do this on a horizontal surface, so the safety pins can all be put in facing the same direction. That way they can be removed more easily while you are stabilizing the outside edges with machine quilting.

COMPLETING THE HEIRLOOM EFFECT

■ Upon finishing a quilt I put it through the gentle cycle in the washing machine using cold water and Orvus® paste or Syntrapol®. Afterwards the quilt is blocked (gently flattened and straightened by patting it by hand) on a cotton sheet on the carpet in my studio, where it air dries in one or two days

depending on the humidity in the air. The quilt sandwich will shrink one to two inches in comparison to the quilt top, depending on the type of batting that was used.

■ Syntrapol® is the detergent of choice if there still are problems with colors bleeding despite washing all fabrics before using them.

■ Do not panic when you see the backing showing through in the wet quilt or when you see needle holes from your stitching in the wet quilt: both will disappear when the quilt has dried. So will the small holes from the safety pins.

■ As soon as my quilts are dry, they go directly from the floor to the design wall for documentation in slides and pictures, before they are ever folded for storage or shipping.

ABOVE: *Meiny Vermaas-van der Heide pin basting a quilt.*

CATTY-WAMPUS LOG CABIN
BY CARYL BRYER FALLERT

When I was a young child, Catty-wampus was a slang expression used occasionally to describe something that was skewed, any which way, or out of square. This is how I describe the individual blocks in this variation on the traditional Log Cabin pattern. The construction is based upon the traditional Log Cabin technique. Instead of squares or rectangles, however, I have used quadrilaterals in which no two sides are the same length, and no two quadrilaterals in the quilt are the same size.

The outlines of the blocks were drawn full size on a large piece of paper. They were created by simply drawing non-horizontal and non-vertical lines across the paper pattern. I wrote notes on each quadrilateral indicating the colors and the light or dark areas of each edge. Lights and darks interact with each

other along the edges of the blocks, creating an overall design, just as they do in the traditional versions of Log Cabin.

A rectangle of turquoise fabric was positioned near the center of each quadrilateral, and strips of leftover scrap fabrics were sewn, folded back, and pressed, around the edges of the rectangle until the paper quadrilateral was covered. A quarter inch seam allowance was added to the fabric, and the blocks were sewn together along the edge of the paper. When all the blocks were assembled, the paper was removed.

The machine quilting was done freehand, with no marking, in a random, meander pattern. Clear nylon filament was used on the top because I was quilting over a wide range of colors and values.

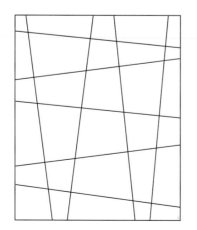

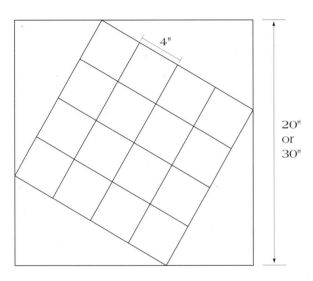

FIG. 1

FREE-PIECED DESIGNS
BY KEIKO GOKE

There is no need to make such a big quilt as my INCLINED LOG CABIN. For example, you can plan to make each Log Cabin 4 inches square and the whole size 20 to 30 inches square (FIG. 1).

Another example is shown here. First you make four blocks of Log Cabin patches without templates (by free piecing) and make each block 20 inches square by incorporating triangles around the Log Cabin blocks (FIG. 2). It's interesting to assemble four big blocks.

If you find it difficult to make the design without templates, draw one segment as in FIG. 3. After sewing four blocks of Log Cabin patches, sew them together to form a square and mark the points. Then incorporate four triangles around them.

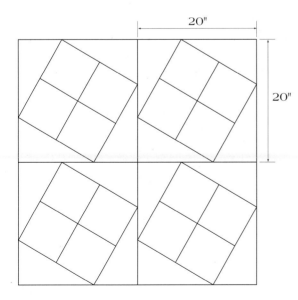

FIG. 2

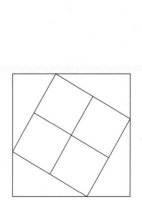

FIG. 3

ADDING CHECKERBOARD STRIPS AND COUCHING
BY BARBARA OLIVER HARTMAN

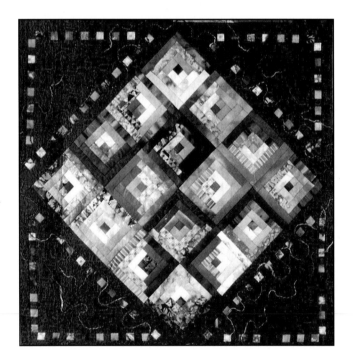

ABOVE: *JUST BECAUSE, detail.*
RIGHT: *Graph to plan your own couching placement.*

JUST BECAUSE is composed of traditional design Log Cabin blocks. Basically, all of the Log Cabin blocks are 7 inches square, with the ones in the center turned on point. The corners around the center section were constructed starting with a 14" square cut into triangles.

Then strips of the fabrics from the interior Log Cabin blocks were sewn, alternating with strips from the background so that every other fabric is background. Strips were cut from this created fabric and then sewn together end to end until there was enough "checkerboard" strip to go around the triangles. After the strips were sewn on, a strip of the background fabric was added so that the finished corner triangles would be 21 inches.

After sewing the corners onto the center blocks, the center portion of the quilt should measure 42 inches. The quilt is completed by sewing six Log Cabin blocks to the top and bottom of the quilt and eight blocks on each side.

The quilt is machine quilted. I stitched in the ditch around the blocks and all of the "logs." The corners are quilted with the feed dogs down and using a meandering stitch.

One of the most distinctive features of the quilt is probably the decorative couched yarn. The yarn is sewn on in a random fashion to soften the straight lines of the quilt. It wouldn't have to be sewn exactly where I placed it – it offers a great opportunity for creative design.

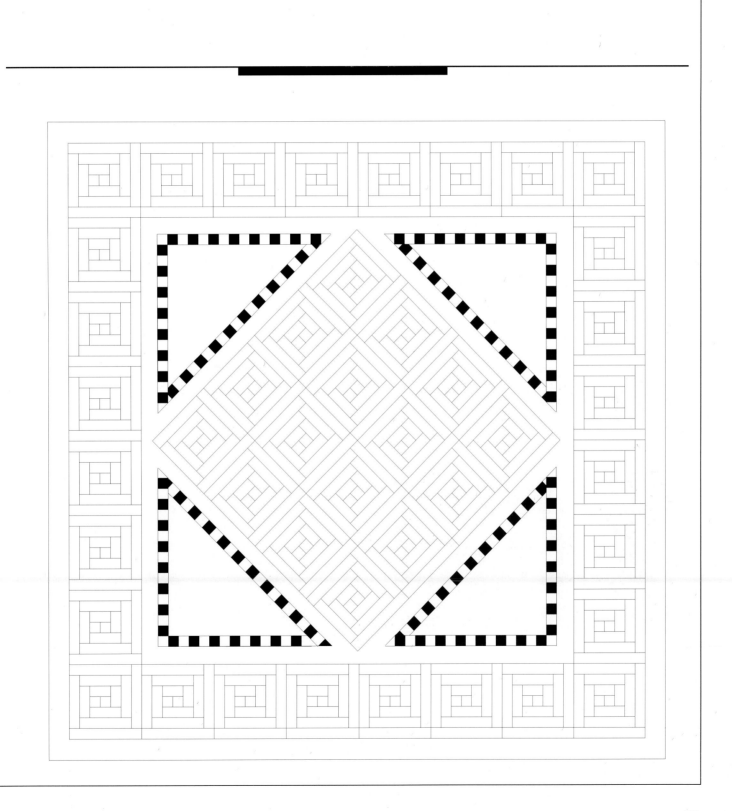

CREATING FABRIC PORTRAITS
BY NANCY S. BROWN

ABOVE: *Photo of the pattern I drew for the quilt. The squares represent where the Log Cabin blocks would be placed.*
LEFT: *Photos of penguins that I took at the San Francisco Zoo. None of the penguins are the exact penguins seen in the quilt because I wanted them in specific poses. But I did use these photos as references to create my own penguins. (Elvis and his guitar were also created using several different photos.)*

Creating fabric portraits, whether animals or people, can be a lot of fun. Animals are probably easier to do than people because whether you choose to make them realistic, stylistic, or cartoonish they will probably be recognizable as the animals you are trying to portray. People are a little trickier because we all know so well what people look like that we can intuitively tell when something is not quite right with a portrait, even if we can't always tell exactly what it is. With a little practice though, anyone can learn to create portraits in fabric. The most important thing to remember is to have fun with them and not worry too much whether or not your portraits are perfect.

Whether you choose to portray animals or people, here are a few tips to get you started:

■ Choose a subject that inspires you and study it closely. With animals, a trip to the zoo or aquarium or park will teach you a lot about the size, shape, color, and movement of your subject. A little people watching will help a great deal in designing your people quilt.

■ Choose a subject that has a lot of contrast for your first portrait. A black and white panda, for instance, will be easier to do than an all-brown grizzly bear. It will also be easier to use a high contrast black and white photo of a person for your design rather than the actual person or a color photo. This will make it easier to tell where the light, medium, and dark values for your design are, and it will simplify your fabric choices.

■ Make your portraits large enough that individual pattern pieces will be manageable in size when you're working with fabrics.

■ When it comes to details, I often think that less is better. I don't think that it is necessary to include every shadow, wrinkle, hair, or fold of clothing. If you represent or suggest the most distinctive details, the viewer's mind will fill in the rest. To find the main details or shadows, look at your subject and squint your eyes. This will help eliminate the less important details and will help you see the light, medium, and dark values of your subject.

■ Many of the details of your portraits can be created with printed fabric. There are a lot of nice prints that can add texture to your quilt and give the impression of hair, fur, feathers, or scales.

■ Profiles are easier to start with because most of the detail is created in the outline and you don't need to add much more.

■ To learn more about portraits go to the local library, bookstore, or art supply store. There are many drawing books available on both animals and people. Anatomy books can also be very helpful.

RAW-EDGE APPLIQUÉ
BY MICHELE M. DUELL

Tips on raw edge appliqué:

- Decide what type of raw edge is desired. Possibilities include a pinked edge, a torn edge, or an edge cut with scissors.
- Secure the appliqué pieces to the background. I usually use a glue stick. I sometimes use a fusible backing or a powdered fusible glue. Pins can be difficult because once sewing begins, I usually don't want to stop to take them out. I have also put a piece of Solvy® over an appliqué and held the whole piece of work together with a spring type embroidery hoop. The Solvy® is washed out after the stitching is completed.
- Stabilize the appliqué and the background fabric if needed. Iron-on products are useful for this, but in a pinch, a sheet of paper or an extra layer of fabric will do the trick. The idea is to prevent the stitches from drawing together too tightly on the underside.
- I always appliqué using free-motion stitching. Drop or cover the feed dogs and adjust the tension, experimenting on a scrap of the same weight (using the same number of layers).
- Zigzag or straight stitches can be used, but with practice, many machine embroidery techniques, fancy machine stitches (the built-in kind), and even double needles can be used effectively.
- Any thread will work, as long as you are willing to find the proper needle and tension setting needed to make it work. My philosophy is that if the stitching is going to show, why be shy? Use thread that will make a statement.

FULL-SIZE PATTERN
FOR EXPERIMENTING

Patterns from the Quilts

MAKING GEESE IN THE BARN
BY CHARLOTTE ROACH

Using the grid below, plan your own GEESE IN THE BARN quilt. Use the patterns on page 74 to cut the Flying Geese elements and the Log Cabin centers and cut 1½" fabric strips (finished width 1") to piece the Log Cabin blocks. You might also want to make your quilt two-sided as I did. A cutting diagram for my pieced quilt back is found on page 75.

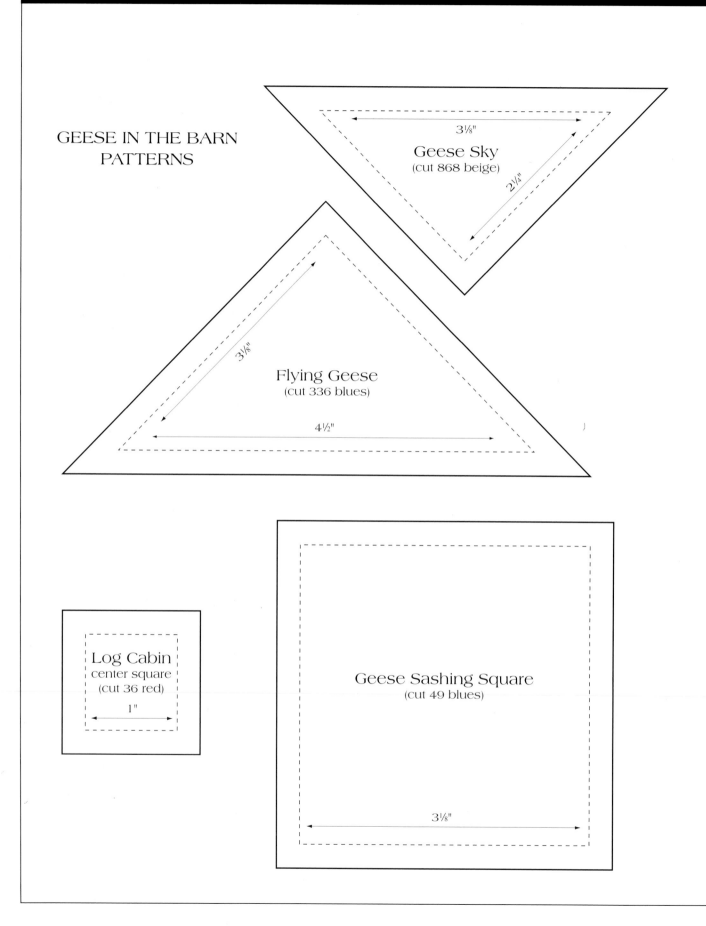

GEESE IN THE BARN
PATTERNS

Geese Sky
(cut 868 beige)

3⅛"

2¼"

Flying Geese
(cut 336 blues)

3⅛"

4½"

Geese Sashing Square
(cut 49 blues)

3⅛"

Log Cabin
center square
(cut 36 red)

1"

GEESE IN THE BARN
CUTTING DIAGRAM – QUILT BACK

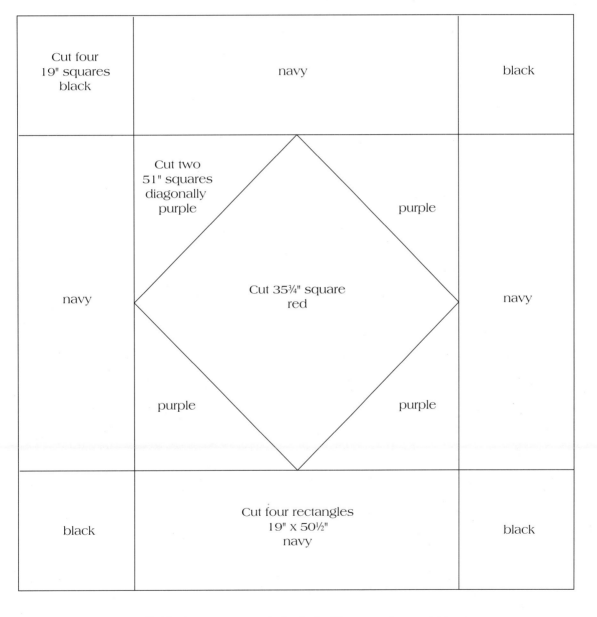

Cut four
19" squares
black

navy

black

Cut two
51" squares
diagonally
purple

purple

navy

Cut 35¾" square
red

navy

purple

purple

black

Cut four rectangles
19" x 50½"
navy

black

Cutting measurements include ½" seam allowances

BUTTERFLIES ARE FREE
BY LOIS MONIESON

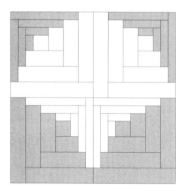

FIG. 1

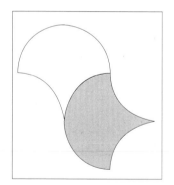

FIG. 2

When I start to design a quilt I usually start with the fabric. I search through books and magazines for ideas and to make sure I don't copy directly from anyone else.

I don't use a computer but I do use copies of blocks to make cut and paste mock-ups of different possibilities. My final quilt layout is shown on page 77.

For BUTTERFLIES ARE FREE I used a 5½" block. I finished the blocks for the borders first and put them on my design wall. The center clamshells are cut from 49 different fabrics. I needed to repeat 22 of these fabrics for the half clamshells.

Four uneven Log Cabin (FIG. 1) blocks were required to make each clamshell (full-size pattern on page 78). Besides the clamshell color four other colors from interlocking clamshells had to be decided on before I could piece even one block. To plan my interlocking color arrangement I cut out a clamshell from cheesecloth and pinned all the precut logs need for one clamshell to the cheesecloth. These pinned together clamshells were arranged and re-arranged on my design wall until I decided on a pleasing arrangement (FIG. 2). The logs were unpinned from

each cheesecloth clamshell and sewn together.

When I quilt I use a 12" hoop. I basted the layers together using a two to three inch grid. I do not pre-mark quilt tops before basting. To mark BUTTERFLIES ARE FREE I cut templates from heavy plastic template material. I traced each segment on clear self-adhesive shelf plastic. The clamshell rings were cut out and placed on the quilt using the diagram provided (page 79). Some pinning is required and new rings are needed from time to time.

Each appliquéd butterfly is a little quilt. I used the method Ann Boyce calls "three-dimensional appliqué" described in her book *Appliqué the Ann Boyce Way*.

Each butterfly includes a top layer, cotton batting, and a backing. I quilted each butterfly by hand with sashiko thread. I satin stitched around the edges of each block. I cut away close to the satin stitching. Placing tear-away stabilizer behind each butterfly, I satin stitched around cut edge.

Each butterfly was attached to the top of the quilt just underneath the slightly rippled edge to give the appearance that it is just lightly resting on the quilt.

BUTTERFLIES ARE FREE

Final quilt layout.

BUTTERFLIES ARE FREE
PATTERN

Shown at 100%.

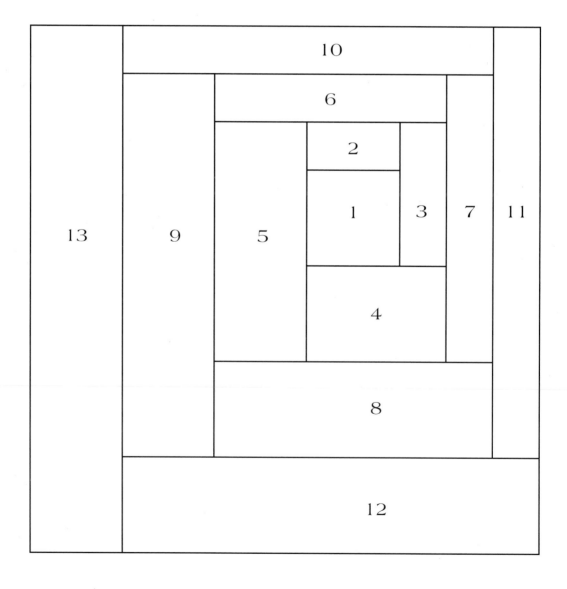

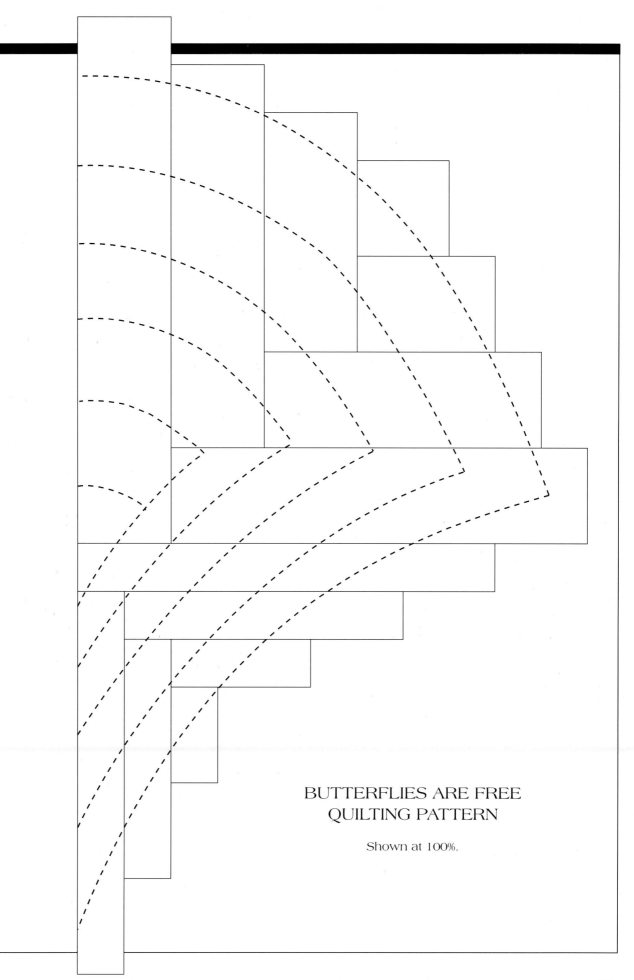

BUTTERFLIES ARE FREE
QUILTING PATTERN

Shown at 100%.

MAKING "EXUBERANT" LOG CABIN BLOCKS
BY WANDA S. HANSON

As difficult as my quilt EXU-BERANCE looks, it has a fairly simple plan. There are only two kinds of blocks. Eighteen have larger centers and three logs on each side. The other 17 have small centers and as many logs as it took to get the blocks big enough to cut out an 11" square.

The 18 blocks started out with 3" squares for centers. I then angled the first 3" wide strip right sides together with the center square and sewed (FIG. 1), trimming away the little corner of the square and pressing the pieces flat (FIG. 2). I added the next 3" wide strip (FIG. 3), angling it again, never using the same degree of angle twice, and sewed. I continued to add strips (FIG. 4), angling each one a little differently until I had three logs on each side. I then pressed it one final time and cut an 11" square out of it, getting the most interesting angle on the outside strips as I could (FIG. 5).

The 17 blocks were made from scraps, in any size and shape with the same general idea as the other blocks. Any-time the block became boring, I added the new strip at a bigger angle. Sometimes I sewed several strips to one side before going on to the next side.

In designing the overall quilt, I alternated simpler blocks with the more involved ones, so that there would not be an appearance of overall confusion. The quilting design needed to be kept fairly simple, so I just used the idea of zebra stripes, from the border fabric. I machine quilted two stripes through each block in both directions, using a black-to-gray variagated rayon thread.

FIG. 1

FIG. 2

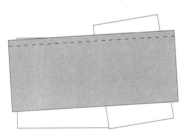

FIG. 3

FIG. 4

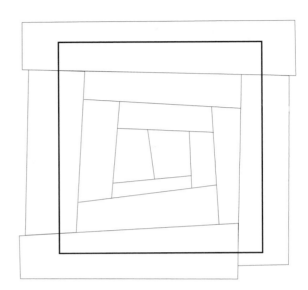

FIG. 5

EXUBERANCE, single block.

FOUNDATION PIECING
BY ALLISON LOCKWOOD

To design my quilt I copied the Pineapple block on a photocopier, and then taped the blocks together. I used my children's crayons to color the blocks in. After making three quilt designs, I chose my favorite and that became my "map." I started making blocks from the center of the quilt and worked out. My color choices were already made, but actual fabric choices were made as I went along.

For the construction on SPELLBOUND I used purchased 9" tear-away foundations called "Perfect Pineapples" (C & T Publishing). On other quilts I've used foundations made by Quilting Techniques, Inc. that are a combination of Log Cabin and Pineapple variations on one sheet. It's very expedient and convenient to use these. If you want to save money, do a different size, or make a customized block, I've found that typing or graph paper work fine. You can either draw the sewing lines on each block or use a copy machine for larger quilts.

I used the piecing method as described by Dixie Haywood and Jane Hall in the book *Perfect Pineapples*. For SPELLBOUND, the fabric was placed on top of the foundation sheet. This placement feels *normal*. I've also tried placing the fabric under the foundation and sewn directly on the paper. This method feels very awkward at first but is more accurate than the first method. After completion of a block or two, both methods will seem easy.

There are a few pointers that will help you sew Log Cabin blocks on paper foundations:

■ Use a pencil to write a description of each fabric (dots, pink, ugly) on the area of the foundation paper in which it is to be placed. This prevents sewing fabric in the wrong place.

■ Use a very short machine stitch. I set my stitch length between 1 and 2 on my machine. A small stitch will make the paper easier to remove when the quilt top is completed. Also, tearing the paper off will put some strain on the seam so it's important that a loose stitch is not used.

■ Leave all the foundations on until your top is completed and you're ready to baste.

■ Fill a spray bottle full of water. Spray the paper on back of the block really well before attempting to remove the paper. It will come off a lot easier.

■ It took three weeks to remove the paper from my quilt. Be patient about the time it takes to remove the paper. A Pineapple Log Cabin not sewn on a foundation will probably end up in your UFO (unfinished objects) pile!

■ If your strips aren't sewn exactly on the sewing line of the foundation, don't worry about it. There is one exception, though. Make sure you are sewing perfectly on the line where the seams come to the outer edge of the block. If you're off here, when you sew your blocks together the seams won't match.

PINEAPPLE LOG CABIN
FOUNDATION PIECING PATTERN

Shown at 50%.

DESIGNING WITH THE PINEAPPLE LOG CABIN BLOCK

What makes the Pineapple Log Cabin block so fascinating is the infinite ways you can change the appearance of the block by manipulating colors.

I've colored in blocks to demonstrate the design possibilities. First I've colored the blocks the way most people think of as a Pineapple (FIG. 1). Then I've colored in blocks as used in SPELLBOUND (FIG. 2). Lastly I've made some new colorations (FIG. 3). Any of these blocks can be repeated in a quilt or can be used in combinations to make a complex-looking puzzle.

Other ideas include mixing Pineapple and non-pineapple Log Cabin blocks, using two different sized blocks, or placing all the blocks on point.

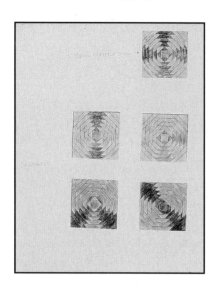

FIG. 1

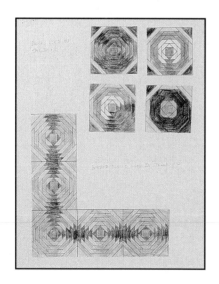

FIG. 2

FIG. 3

SPELLBOUND

Use this grid to plan your own quilt based on this design.

LOG CABIN SQUARED
BY NANCY TAYLOR

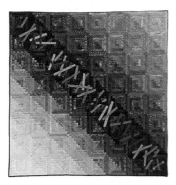

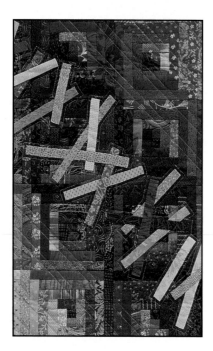

LOG CABIN 1991. 53" x 53".
Nancy Taylor 1991.
Full quilt (top) and detail (above).

The block I used has ¾" logs, is 6¾" finished, and is 7¼" with seam allowances. To draw the paper foundation, draw the block on accurate graph paper, as seen when finished (with seam lines drawn, rather than seam allowance edges). Extend the log outlines or seam lines ¼" above and below their intersections. Indicate on the pattern by shading which logs are dark. Draw a star in the center square. (See page 88 for my full-size pattern.)

Print the pattern on a copier. Two blocks will fit snugly on an 8½" x 14" sheet; you can cut the blocks apart to use them. Make sure the copier that you choose will not distort the image in either direction; superimpose the original onto the copy, then hold it up to a light to compare the two outlines.

Cut fabric strips across the width of fabric which has been folded in fourths. Cut strips ⅛" wider than the usual width desired. The logs in my pattern are ¾" wide finished. Ordinarily they would be cut 1¼" wide including seam allowances. If an extra ⅛" is added, making the cut strips 1⅜" wide, there are fewer problems when sewing from the opposite side of a paper pattern.

The strips of fabric are stacked side-by-side in two rows. One row contains light fabrics, the other row darker fabrics.

I compose each block before I sew by selecting which fabric I want to use for each side – dark and light. I cut two 1⅜" squares, one dark for the center and one light for the first log. Then, with the help of a paper that is marked with the length of each successive log, I cut each fabric strip slightly longer than the length indicated on my "chart." I lay the logs out in the order in which they will be sewn.

All sewing is done on the lines on the paper pattern, but all fabrics are arranged on the reverse side of the paper. To begin the block, place a 1⅜" light square face down on a 1⅜" dark square, which will be the center square of the block. Hold the paper pattern up to a light source, with the Log Cabin design facing you. Put the two squares on the back of the paper with the wrong side of the dark fabric against the paper. Center the shadow of the squares directly over the starred center square on the pattern and distribute the seam allowance evenly around the marked square. Using a fine pin, pin through the paper of the starred square to hold the fabric pieces in place for sewing.

Before sewing, place a larger sewing machine needle in your machine – nice, new, and sharp. I use a 14 or 90.

Set your machine for smaller stitches. My machine is usually set at around a 2 or 2½ stitch length. For sewing on a paper foundation, I reduce the length to 1½.

By using a larger needle and taking stitches that are closer together, the eventual paper removal is much easier.

With the fabric pieces in place on the wrong side of the foundation pattern, place the paper pattern under the presser foot, face up, with the fabric pieces underneath. Starting ¼" above the seam outline, sew along the seam line indicated between the dark square and the light square on your pattern. When finished, cut threads, remove pins, and turn the paper over. Fold the top square right side out, finger press, then press the seam lightly with a dry iron.

Place a large piece of muslin on top of your ironing surface.

The photocopy ink will often transfer to your ironing board since you will be pressing with the copy side down.

After pressing, place the next fabric strip face down over the first two fabrics. Again, hold the paper up to a light source, fabric side facing away from you. Align the shadow of the fabric strip with its seam allowance extending ¼" outside the photocopied seam line. Pin in place with the pin parallel to the seam line, and in the center of the strip. Sew as before, beginning and ending ¼" above and below the intersecting seam line. As logs get longer, it may be necessary to pin at the top and bottom of each log. Cut the end of each strip to fit by folding it back against itself ¼" above the seamline and trimming carefully with scissors.

When the block is complete, press well. Trim by rotary cutting ¼" outside the block outline all around the pattern.

Remove the paper from each outside perimeter log. The remaining paper can be removed after the blocks are sewn together.

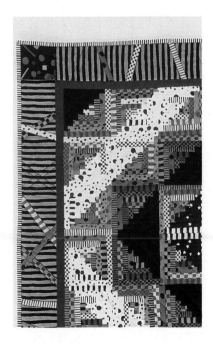

LOG CABIN 1992. 35" x 35".
Nancy Taylor 1992.
Full quilt (top) and detail (above).

LOG CABIN SQUARED
PAPER FOUNDATION PATTERN

Shown at 100%.

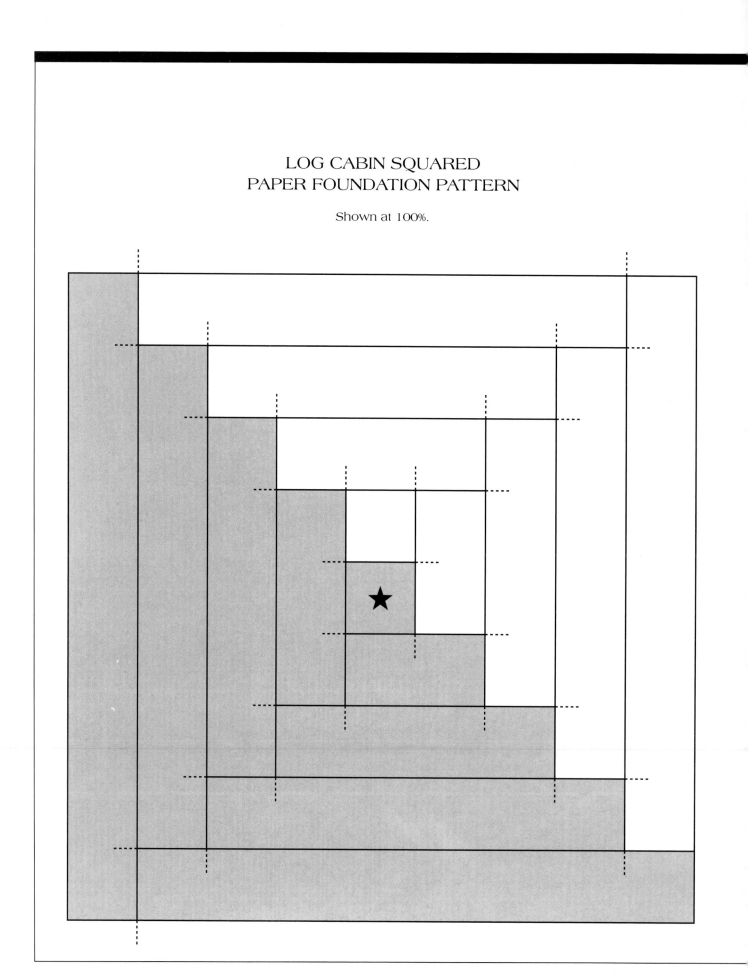

EYE OF THE STORM
BY DEANNA D. DISON

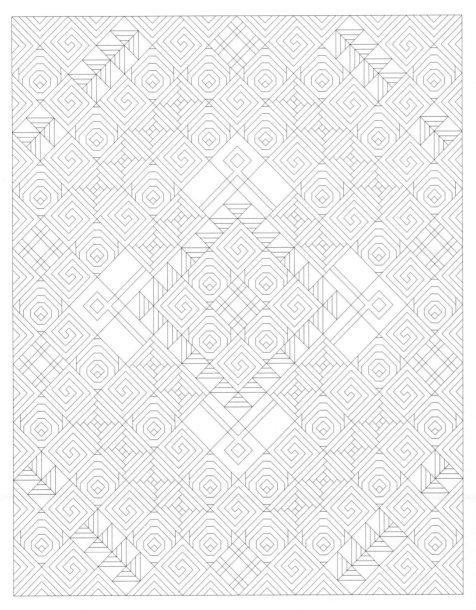

To develop a quilt design I frequently draw a grid like the one shown and color it in many different ways before arriving at the one I think will really work, as you will note from photos of some of my many working drawings. The design for this quilt involved seven different blocks, all based on some lines of the traditional Log Cabin block. Full-size patterns for these 6" and 3" blocks follow. Color in the grid and create your own version of EYE OF THE STORM.

RIGHT: Examples of several working drawings I tried before finding the one that worked.

Final color sketch before choosing fabrics.

EYE OF THE STORM PATTERN

Add seam allowances.

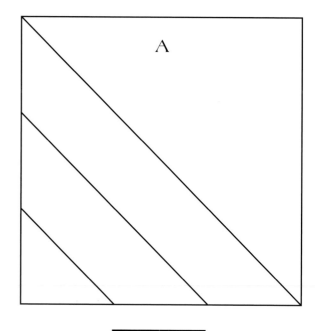

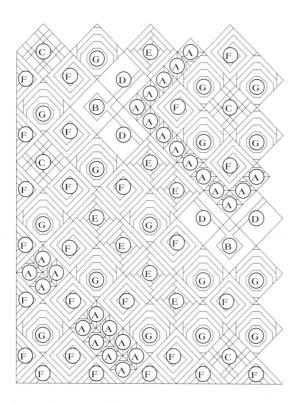

Pattern placement guide.

EYE OF THE STORM
PATTERN

Add seam allowances.

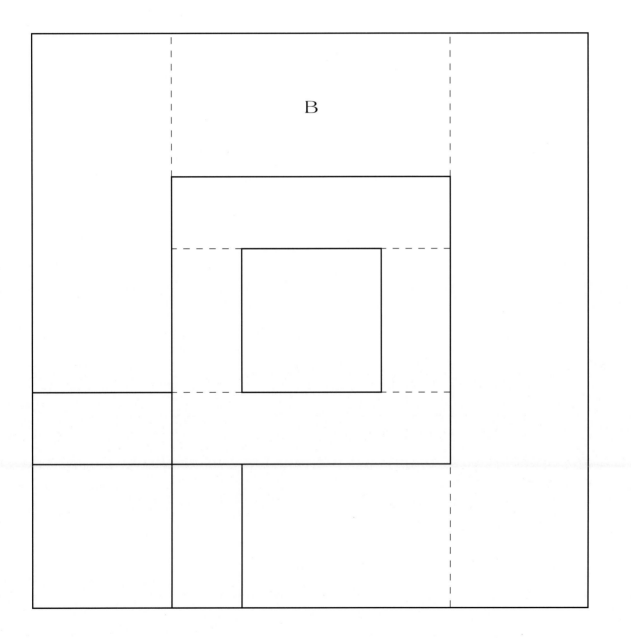

EYE OF THE STORM
PATTERN

Add seam allowances.

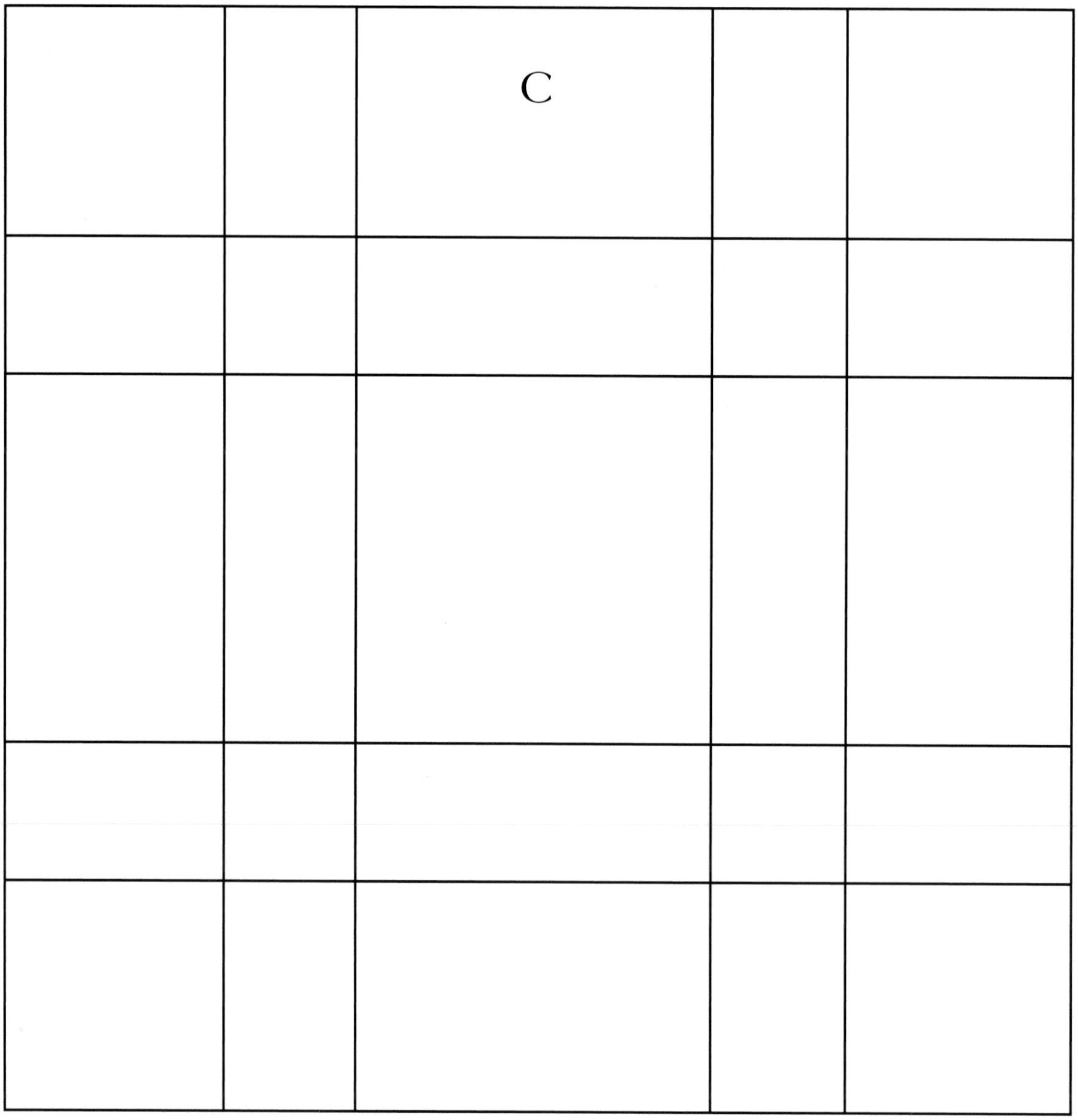

C

DEANNA D. DISON

EYE OF THE STORM
PATTERN

Add seam allowances.

D

EYE OF THE STORM
PATTERN

Add seam allowances.

EYE OF THE STORM
PATTERN

Add seam allowances.

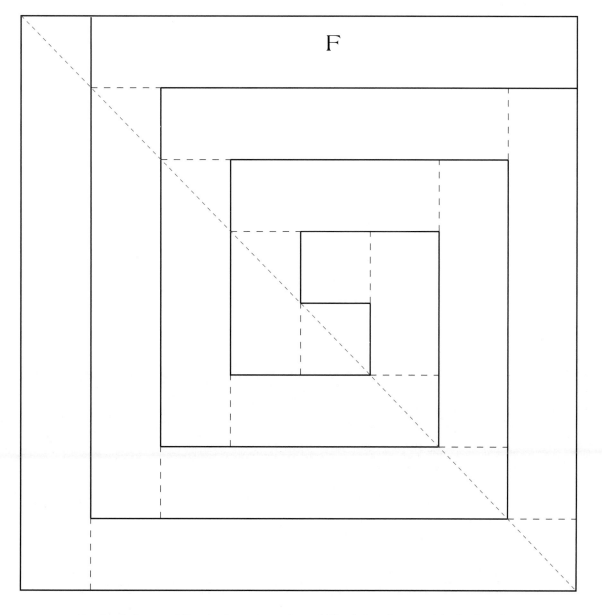

F

Dashed diagonal line indicates section of Block F to be used in the border.

EYE OF THE STORM
PATTERN

Add seam allowances.

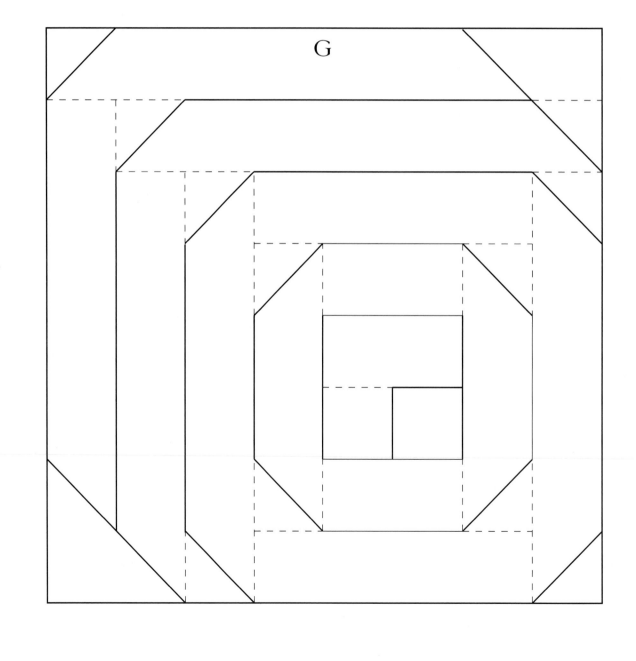

G

COMBINING FABRICS AND LOG CABIN PATTERNS
BY DIANE TURSCAK

My quilts are often based on a scrap concept. I have a rule that I can buy any fabric I want, but I only buy ¼ to ½ yard pieces. This is because I am an incorrigible fabricaholic, and own half a store's worth. I would go bankrupt otherwise. I will buy larger pieces, of course, for the borders and backing. When I start a quilt, I just go into my fabric stash and start pulling fabric. I plan as I go, and have no real preconceived notions of the total objective. Because of the way I work, I usually do not have to worry about running out; I can just add another fabric. My quilts evolve. Sometimes a quilt will sit and wait for a few weeks, while I mull over what will come next.

The quilt layout and pattern sources I used are provide on page 98. I used the flip and sew method for the houses, and just went into my scrap bag. I made three blocks as shown on the instructions from Mary Golden and then turned the paper piecing blocks over and sewed two more on the wrong side. For the Pineapple block I suggest using two inch strips as flip and sew requires a little more fabric than normal piecing because things do not always end up where you think they will. Placing one of the house blocks in the center of the Pineapple design I worked from there.

Then I made four traditional Log Cabin blocks. My house was light looking so I started with a dark strip first. Working my way around the block, I added two darks, then two lights, two darks, then two lights until I had surrounded the house four times.

Then I made four Courthouse Steps blocks. I cut the center squares and then cut 8 to 10 strips of light and 8 to 10 strips of dark. As above, if the center is dark, start with the light strips, working left side, right side, then a dark strip and add top and bottom strips. Work in this manner around the center five times. The nine blocks are put together to form the central design.

I then took four strips of light blue and surrounded the nine blocks. Then I added the next border. I worked backwards, first making the 24 willow tree blocks and then figuring the border size, and corner blocks.

You will need 8 to 10 strips of "dirt" fabric, and 3 to 4 strips of brown for the tree trunks, and about 36 to 40 strips of assorted greens. I usually only cut the length that I need to start with, such as for the trunk of the tree, and add my strips and clip. If this method is used, it saves a lot of planning, but you had better cut and sew accurately. I never use templates if I can help it. You can cut the individual pieces with your ruler and mat, or do as I do and sew on the strips and clip or rotary cut with a small square as you go. Attach the blocks in rows. Two rows with five blocks each to two opposite sides, and two rows with seven blocks each to the other two sides.

Add a border, layer, and quilt! I lap quilt, and don't use a hoop, but I do it with the whole quilt in one piece.

CABINS IN THE WILLOWS
QUILT DIAGRAM

			63"			
Tree	Tree	Tree	Tree	Tree	Tree	Tree
Tree						Tree
Tree	Traditional Log Cabin with House	Courthouse Steps	Traditional Log Cabin with House reversed			Tree
Tree	Courthouse Steps	Pineapple with House	Courthouse Steps			Tree
Tree	Traditional Log Cabin with House	Courthouse Steps	Traditional Log Cabin with House reversed			Tree
Tree						Tree
Tree	Tree	Tree	Tree	Tree	Tree	Tree

(Inner block dimension: 36")

PATTERNS: *Branching Out Tree Quilts* by Carol Ann Palmer,
That Patchwork Place.™

PATTERNS: *Flip & Sew Paper Templates for Machine Piecing,*
by Mary B. Golden, Quilting Techniques, Inc.™

SUPERNOVA
BY BARBARA T. KAEMPFER

This quilt is a construction of uneven blocks. Every block has different angles on each corner and the side length differs, too. To construct such a quilt one has to draw the whole quilt in its original size.

Printing the original design for this quilt, which includes 100 different blocks was impossible, but the design can also be done with even blocks. To make a quilt similar to SUPERNOVA (but with even blocks) one can use an even block with 5" sides.

The 5" block on page 100 can be copied and used as a foundation sheet for as many blocks as you need. To make a quilt the size of SUPERNOVA, you would use 100 blocks.

The fabric is sewn directly on the paper foundation. It is very important to keep in mind that the resulting blocks will be a mirror image of the design. If the design for the final quilt shows blocks with a clockwise twist, the paper foundation needs to be drawn with a counterclockwise twist.

A center square with ¼" seam allowance is cut. The centerpiece is placed in such a way that it covers all the lines of the center on the paper foundation. Then the sewing is done from the center outwards, using strips cut 1" wide. Before ironing, the seams are trimmed.

If you wish to create your own design, you can use the pattern for templates. Step-by-step instructions for this approach will be given in my book being published by AQS.

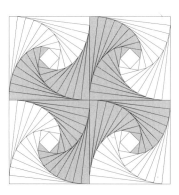

ABOVE RIGHT: *Using this block, you can make quilts with various traditional settings, such as Barn Raising, Straight Furrows, Light and Dark, and many more.*
RIGHT: *Barn Raising or Straight Furrows layout.*

SUPERNOVA
PATTERN

Shown at 100%.

SUPERNOVA

Use this grid to plan your own quilt based on the even block quilt, ¼ of quilt.

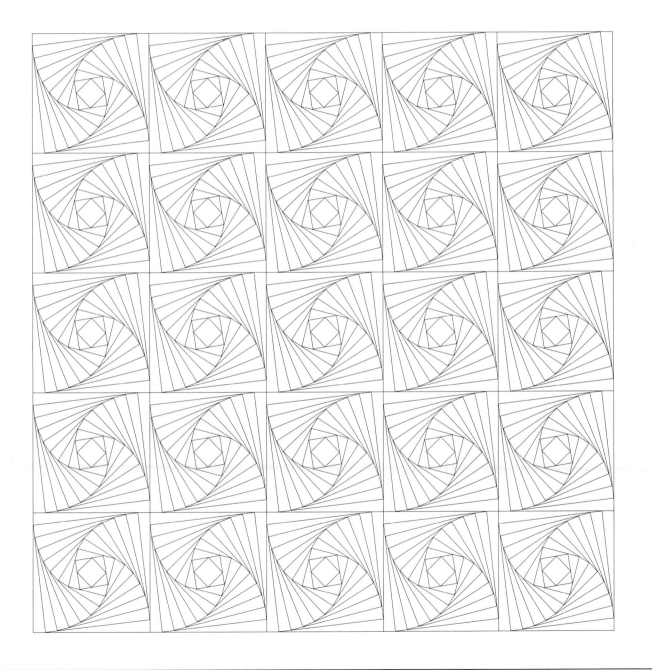

SUPERNOVA

Shown with even blocks.

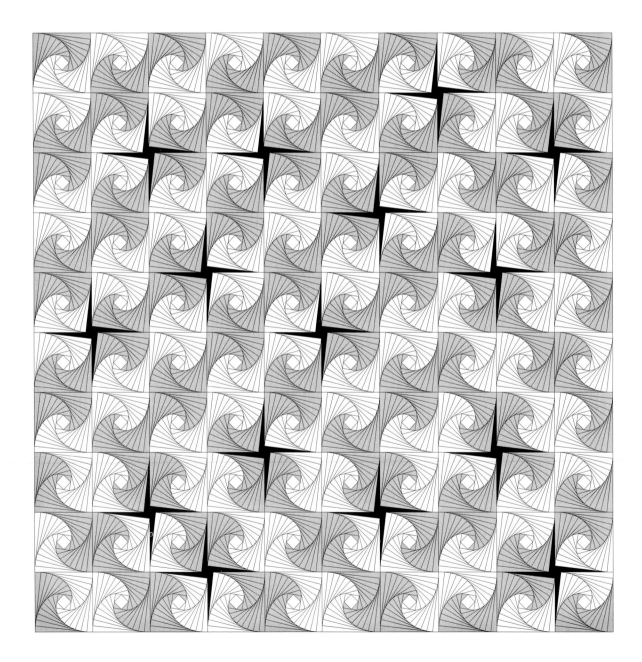

BLOCK A PATTERN
Shown at 50%.

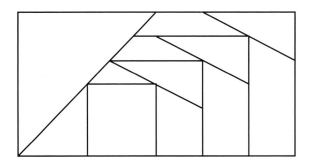

BLOCK C PATTERN (Border)
Shown at 50%.

QUASARS
BY LAURA MURRAY

Working with off-center versions of the Pineapple Log Cabin block, I created a set of four and then let the quilt develop from there. I basically worked with the three blocks shown on this page, rotating them and combining them in various ways. As you can see on the grid (page 104), this design created with only three blocks looks very complex, and offers great opportunities for experimenting with color. Try your own hand at achieving a variety of effects by using tracing paper over the grid to experiment with various ways of interpreting the design in color. You may find one you like so much you can't resist making it in fabrics.

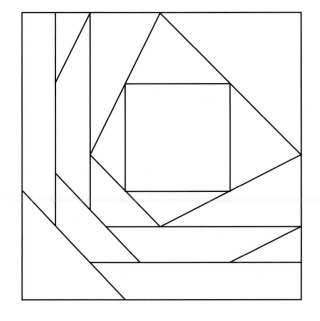

BLOCK B PATTERN
Shown at 50%.

QUASARS

Use this grid to plan your own QUASARS quilt.

FOUR AND TWENTY BLACKBIRDS DIVIDED BY TWO
BY CATHERINE MCINTEE

This quilt combines published patterns, traditional Log Cabin blocks, elements inspired by an antique quilt, and my own designs. Most of the center block was taken from a pattern on page 79 of Jeanna Kimball's book *Red and Green – An Appliqué Tradition*. I replaced her birds and reduced the block size slightly so it would fit in the area I needed. I then used elements from the original block to design the 10 alternate blocks with the single bird, and to create the 14 set triangles with the branch only.

I got the idea for the sawteeth around the Log Cabin blocks in the Ohio Quilt Search book, entitled *Quilts in Community – Ohio's Traditions*. Page 39 of the book shows a great antique quilt made by Amanda Fulmer prior to her death in 1919. Although the centers of Amanda's blocks are more like crazy patchwork than Log Cabin piecing, there is a similarity which I find intriguing.

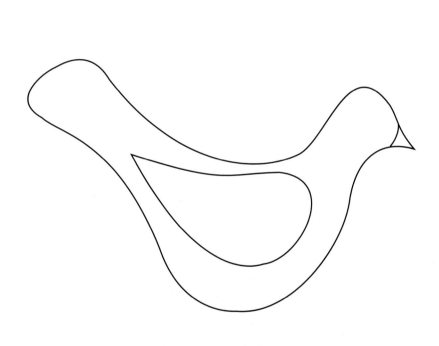

FOUR AND TWENTY BLACKBIRDS DIVIDED BY TWO PATTERN

Shown at 100%.

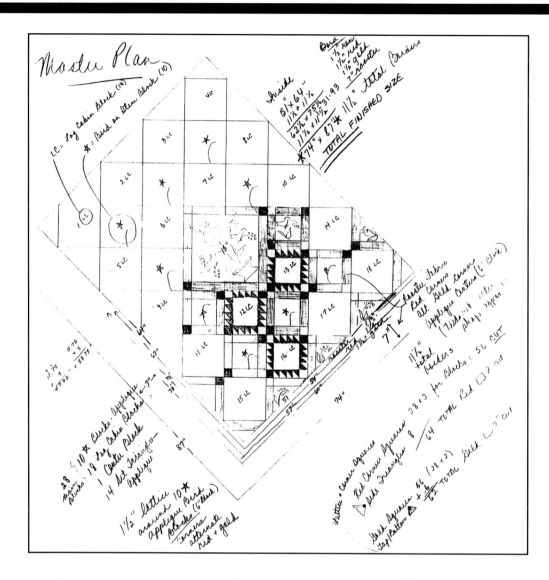

Master Plan

ABOVE: *Example of how I designed the quilt before starting to work.*
LEFT: *Photo of the finished quilt.*

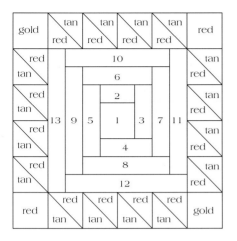

Pattern guide for Sawtooth Log Cabin blocks.

FOUR & TWENTY BLACKBIRDS
DIVIDED BY TWO
PATTERN

Shown at 100%.

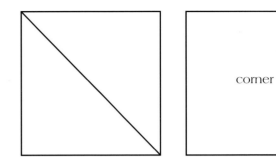

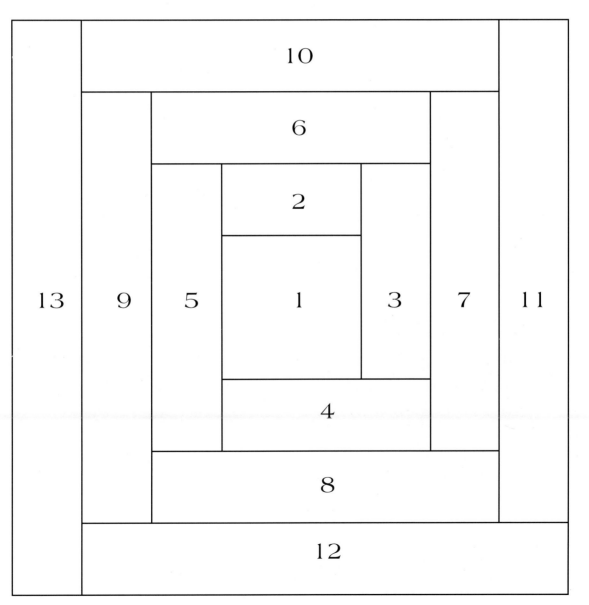

The Quiltmakers

Brown, Nancy S. 22–23, 70–71

Dison, Deanna D. 24–25, 89–96

Duell, Michele M. 26–27, 72

Fahl, Ann 20–21, 62–63

Fallert, Caryl Bryer 28–29, 66

Goke, Keiko 14–15, 67

Hanson, Wanda S. 30–31, 80–81

Hartman, Barbara Oliver 32–33, 68–69

Kaempfer, Barbara T. 18–19, 99–102

Lockwood, Allison 34–35, 82–85

McIntee, Catherine 36–37, 105–107

Monieson, Lois 38–39, 76–79

Murray, Laura 16–17, 103–104

Roach, Charlotte 40–41, 73–75

Smith, Cynthia 42–43, 61

Taylor, Nancy 44–45, 86–88

Turscak, Diane 46–47, 97–98

Vermaas–van der Heide, Meiny 48–49, 64–65

The Quilts

Butterflies Are Free...38–39

Cabins in the Willows 46–47

Elvis and the Penguins 22–23

Exuberance 30–31

Eye of the Storm...24–25

Four and Twenty Blackbirds Divided by Two 36–37

Geese in the Barn...40–41

Girls at Home, The 26–27

Homage to Mondriaan VII: a GREEN QUILT 48–49

Inclined Log Cabin 14–15

Just Because 32–33

Log Cabin Squared...44–45

Quasars...16–17

Raising a "New Age" Barn..42–43

Skylights..28–29

Spellbound 34–35

Supernova 1994 18–19

Under the Log Cabin Sky..20–21

The Museum

MUSEUM OF THE AMERICAN QUILTER'S SOCIETY
215 Jefferson Street, Paducah, Kentucky

A dream long held by American Quilter's Society founders Bill and Meredith Schroeder and by quilters worldwide was realized on April 25, 1991, when the Museum of the American Quilter's Society (MAQS, pronounced "Max") opened its doors in Paducah, Kentucky. As is stated in brass lettering over the building's entrance, this non-profit institution is dedicated to "honoring today's quilter," by stimulating and supporting the study, appreciation, and development of quiltmaking throughout the world.

The 30,000 square foot facility includes a central exhibition gallery featuring a selection of the 135 quilts by contemporary quiltmakers comprising the museum's permanent collection, and two additional galleries displaying exhibits of antique and contemporary quilts. Lectures, workshops, and other related activities are also held on site, in spacious modern classrooms. A gift and book shop makes available a wide selection of fine crafts and quilt books. The museum is open year-round and is handicapped accessible.

For more information, write: MAQS, P.O. Box 1540, Paducah, KY 42002-1540 or phone: 502-442-8856.

Other MAQS Publications

Contemporary Quilts from The James Collection
Ardis James
#4525: AQS, 1995, 40 pages, 6" x 9", softbound, $12.95.

Double Wedding Ring Quilts: New Quilts from an Old Favorite
Edited by Victoria Faoro
#3870: AQS, 1994, 112 pages, 8½" x 11", softbound, $14.95.

Log Cabin Returns to Kentucky, The: Quilts from the Pilgrim/Roy Collection
Paul D. Pilgrim and Gerald E. Roy
#3329: AQS, 1992, 36 pages, 9" x 7", softbound, $12.95.

Nancy Crow: Quilts and Influences
Nancy Crow
#1981: AQS, 1990, 256 pages, 9" x 12", hardcover, $29.95.

Nancy Crow: Work in Transition
Nancy Crow
#3331: AQS, 1992, 32 pages, 9" x 10", softbound, $12.95.

New Jersey Quilts – 1777 to 1950: Contributions to an American Tradition
The Heritage Quilt Project of New Jersey
#3332: AQS, 1992, 256 pages, 8½" x 11", softbound, $29.95.

Quilts: Old and New, A Similar View
Paul D. Pilgrim and Gerald E. Roy
#3715: AQS, 1993, 40 pages, 8¾" x 8", softbound, $12.95.

Quilts: The Permanent Collection – MAQS
#2257: AQS, 1991, 100 pages, 10" x 6½", softbound, $9.95.

Quilts: The Permanent Collection, Volume II – MAQS
#3793: AQS, 1994, 80 pages, 10" x 6½", softbound, $9.95.

Victorian Quilts, 1875–1900: They Aren't All Crazy
Paul D. Pilgrim and Gerald E. Roy
#3932: AQS, 1994, 64 pages, 6" x 9", softbound, $14.95.

These books can be found in the MAQS bookshop and in local bookstores and
quilt shops. If you are unable to locate a title in your area, you can order by mail from:

American Quilter's Society
P.O. Box 3290, Paducah, KY 42002-3290

Please add $1 for the first book and $.40 for each additional one to cover postage and handling.
International orders please add $1.50 for the first book and $1 for each additional one.

To order by VISA or MASTERCARD call toll-free: 1-800-626-5420 or fax: 1-502-898-8890.

⌘American Quilter's Society⌘
dedicated to publishing books for today's quilters

The following AQS publications are currently available:

- **Adapting Architectural Details for Quilts,** Carol Wagner, #2282: AQS, 1992, 88 pages, softbound, $12.95
- **American Beauties: Rose & Tulip Quilts,** Gwen Marston & Joe Cunningham, #1907: AQS, 1988, 96 pages, softbound, $14.95
- **Appliqué Designs: My Mother Taught Me to Sew,** Faye Anderson, #2121: AQS, 1990, 80 pages, softbound, $12.95
- **Appliqué Patterns from Native American Beadwork Designs,** Dr. Joyce Mori, #3790: AQS, 1994, 96 pages, softbound, $14.95
- **Arkansas Quilts: Arkansas Warmth,** Arkansas Quilter's Guild, Inc., #1908: AQS, 1987, 144 pages, hardbound, $24.95
- **The Art of Hand Appliqué,** Laura Lee Fritz, #2122: AQS, 1990, 80 pages, softbound, $14.95
- **...Ask Helen More About Quilting Designs,** Helen Squire, #2099: AQS, 1990, 54 pages, 17 x 11, spiral-bound, $14.95
- **Award-Winning Quilts & Their Makers, Vol. I: The Best of AQS Shows – 1985-1987,** #2207: AQS, 1991, 232 pages, softbound, $24.95
- **Award-Winning Quilts & Their Makers, Vol. II: The Best of AQS Shows – 1988-1989,** #2354: AQS, 1992, 176 pages, softbound, $24.95
- **Award-Winning Quilts & Their Makers, Vol. III: The Best of AQS Shows – 1990-1991,** #3425: AQS, 1993, 180 pages, softbound, $24.95
- **Award-Winning Quilts & Their Makers, Vol. IV: The Best of AQS Shows – 1992-1993,** #3791: AQS, 1994, 180 pages, softbound, $24.95
- **Celtic Style Floral Appliqué: Designs Using Interlaced Scrollwork,** Scarlett Rose, #3926: AQS, 1995, 128 pages, softbound, $14.95
- **Classic Basket Quilts,** Elizabeth Porter & Marianne Fons, #2208: AQS, 1991, 128 pages, softbound, $16.95
- **A Collection of Favorite Quilts,** Judy Florence, #2119: AQS, 1990, 136 pages, softbound, $18.95
- **Creative Machine Art,** Sharee Dawn Roberts, #2355: AQS, 1992, 142 pages, 9 x 9, softbound, $24.95
- **Dear Helen, Can You Tell Me?...All About Quilting Designs,** Helen Squire, #1820: AQS, 1987, 51 pages, 17 x 11, spiral-bound, $12.95
- **Double Wedding Ring Quilts: New Quilts from an Old Favorite,** #3870: AQS, 1994, 112 pages, softbound, $14.95
- **Dye Painting!,** Ann Johnston, #3399: AQS, 1992, 88 pages, softbound, $19.95
- **Dyeing & Overdyeing of Cotton Fabrics,** Judy Mercer Tescher, #2030: AQS, 1990, 54 pages, softbound, $9.95
- **Encyclopedia of Pieced Quilt Patterns,** compiled by Barbara Brackman, #3468: AQS, 1993, 552 pages, hardbound, $34.95
- **Fabric Postcards: Landmarks & Landscapes • Monuments & Meadows,** Judi Warren, #3846: AQS, 1994, 120 pages, softbound, $22.95
- **Flavor Quilts for Kids to Make: Complete Instructions for Teaching Children to Dye, Decorate & Sew Quilts,** Jennifer Amor, #2356: AQS, 1991, 120 pages, softbound, $12.95
- **From Basics to Binding: A Complete Guide to Making Quilts,** Karen Kay Buckley, #2381: AQS, 1992, 160 pages, softbound, $16.95
- **Fun & Fancy Machine Quiltmaking,** Lois Smith, #1982: AQS, 1989, 144 pages, softbound, $19.95
- **Heirloom Miniatures,** Tina M. Gravatt, #2097: AQS, 1990, 64 pages, softbound, $9.95
- **Infinite Stars,** Gayle Bong, #2283: AQS, 1992, 72 pages, softbound, $12.95
- **The Ins and Outs: Perfecting the Quilting Stitch,** Patricia J. Morris, #2120: AQS, 1990, 96 pages, softbound, $9.95
- **Irish Chain Quilts: A Workbook of Irish Chains & Related Patterns,** Joyce B. Peaden, #1906: AQS, 1988, 96 pages, softbound, $14.95
- **Jacobean Appliqué: Book I, "Exotica,"** Patricia B. Campbell & Mimi Ayars, Ph.D, #3784: AQS, 1993, 160 pages, softbound, $18.95
- **The Judge's Task: How Award-Winning Quilts Are Selected,** Patricia J. Morris, #3904: AQS, 1993, 128 pages, softbound, $19.95
- **Marbling Fabrics for Quilts: A Guide for Learning & Teaching,** Kathy Fawcett & Carol Shoaf, #2206: AQS, 1991, 72 pages, softbound, $12.95
- **More Projects and Patterns: A Second Collection of Favorite Quilts,** Judy Florence, #3330: AQS, 1992, 152 pages, softbound, $18.95
- **Nancy Crow: Quilts and Influences,** Nancy Crow, #1981: AQS, 1990, 256 pages, 9 x 12, hardcover, $29.95
- **Nancy Crow: Work in Transition,** Nancy Crow, #3331: AQS, 1992, 32 pages, 9 x 10, softbound, $12.95
- **New Jersey Quilts – 1777 to 1950: Contributions to an American Tradition,** The Heritage Quilt Project of New Jersey; text by Rachel Cochran, Rita Erickson, Natalie Hart & Barbara Schaffer, #3332: AQS, 1992, 256 pages, softbound, $29.95
- **No Dragons on My Quilt,** Jean Ray Laury with Ritva Laury & Lizabeth Laury, #2153: AQS, 1990, 52 pages, hardcover, $12.95
- **Old Favorites in Miniature,** Tina Gravatt, #3469: AQS, 1993, 104 pages, softbound, $15.95
- **A Patchwork of Pieces: An Anthology of Early Quilt Stories 1845-1940,** complied by Cuesta Ray Benberry and Carol Pinney Crabb, #3333: AQS, 1993, 360 pages, 5½ x 8½, softbound, $14.95
- **Precision Patchwork for Scrap Quilts, Anytime, Anywhere...,** Jeannette Muir, #3928: AQS, 1995, 72 pages, softbound, $12.95
- **Quilt Groups Today: Who They Are, Where They Meet, What They Do, and How to Contact Them – A Complete Guide for 1992-1993,** #3308: AQS, 1992, 336 pages, softbound, $14.95
- **Quilter's Registry,** Lynne Fritz, #2380: AQS, 1992, 80 pages, 5½ x 8½, hardbound, $9.95
- **Quilting Patterns from Native American Designs,** Dr. Joyce Mori, #3467: AQS, 1993, 80 pages, softbound, $12.95
- **Quilting With Style: Principles for Great Pattern Design,** Gwen Marston & Joe Cunningham, #3470: AQS, 1993, 192 pages, hardbound, $24.95
- **Quiltmaker's Guide: Basics & Beyond,** Carol Doak, #2284: AQS, 1992, 208 pages, softbound, $19.95
- **Quilts: The Permanent Collection – MAQS,** #2257: AQS, 1991, 100 pages, 10 x 6½, softbound, $9.95
- **Roots, Feathers & Blooms: 4-Block Quilts, Their History & Patterns, Book I,** Linda Giesler Carlson, #3789: AQS, 1994, 128 pages, softbound, $16.95
- **Seasons of the Heart & Home: Quilts for a Winter's Day,** Jan Patek, #3796: AQS, 1993, 160 pages, softbound, $18.95
- **Seasons of the Heart & Home: Quilts for Summer Days,** Jan Patek, #3761: AQS, 1993, 160 pages, softbound, $18.95
- **Sensational Scrap Quilts,** Darra Duffy Williamson, #2357: AQS, 1992, 152 pages, softbound, $24.95
- **Sets & Borders,** Gwen Marston & Joe Cunningham, #1821: AQS, 1987, 104 pages, softbound, $14.95
- **Show Me Helen...How to Use Quilting Designs,** Helen Squire, #3375: AQS, 1993, 155 pages, softbound, $15.95
- **Somewhere in Between: Quilts and Quilters of Illinois,** Rita Barrow Barber, #1790: AQS, 1986, 78 pages, softbound, $14.95
- **Spike & Zola: Patterns for Laughter...and Appliqué, Painting, or Stenciling,** Donna French Collins, #3794: AQS, 1993, 72 pages, softbound, $9.95
- **Stenciled Quilts for Christmas,** Marie Monteith Sturmer, #2098: AQS, 1990, 104 pages, softbound, $14.95
- **The Stori Book of Embellishing: Great Ideas for Quilts and Garments,** Mary Stori, #3929: AQS, 1994, 96 pages, softbound, $16.95
- **Straight Stitch Machine Appliqué: History, Patterns & Instructions for This Easy Technique,** Letty Martin, #3903: AQS, 1994, 160 pages, softbound, $16.95
- **Striplate Piecing: Piecing Circle Designs with Speed and Accuracy,** Debra Wagner, #3792: AQS, 1994, 168 pages, 9 x 12, hardbound, $24.95
- **Tessellations and Variations: Creating One-Patch & Two-Patch Quilts,** Barbara Ann Caron, #3930: AQS, 1994, 120 pages, softbound, $14.95
- **Three-Dimensional Appliqué and Embroidery Embellishment: Techniques for Today's Album Quilt,** Anita Shackelford, #3788: AQS, 1993, 152 pages, 9 x 12, hardbound, $24.95
- **Time-Span Quilts: New Quilts from Old Tops,** Becky Herdle, #3931: AQS, 1994, 136 pages, softbound, $16.95
- **A Treasury of Quilting Designs,** Linda Goodmon Emery, #2029: AQS, 1990, 80 pages, 14 x 11, spiral-bound, $14.95
- **Tricks with Chintz: Using Large Prints to Add New Magic to Traditional Quilt Blocks,** Nancy S. Breland, #3847: AQS, 1994, 96 pages, softbound, $14.95
- **Wonderful Wearables: A Celebration of Creative Clothing,** Virginia Avery, #2286: AQS, 1991, 184 pages, softbound, $24.95

These books can be found in local bookstores and quilt shops. If you are unable to locate a title in your area, you can order by mail from AQS, P.O. Box 3290, Paducah, KY 42002-3290. Please add $1 for the first book and 40¢ for each additional one to cover postage and handling. (International orders please add $1.50 for the first book and $1 for each additional one.)